WHERE THE DESERT MEETS THE CEDAR

Claudia Mardel

BALBOA.
PRESS
A DIVISION OF HAY HOUSE

Balboa Press books may be ordered through booksellers or by contacting:

Balboa Press
A Division of Hay House
1663 Liberty Drive
Bloomington, IN 47403
www.balboapress.com
1 (877) 407-4847

Because of the dynamic nature of the Internet, any web addresses or
links contained in this book may have changed since publication and
may no longer be valid. The views expressed in this work are solely those
of the author and do not necessarily reflect the views of the publisher,
and the publisher hereby disclaims any responsibility for them.

The author of this book does not dispense medical advice or prescribe the use
of any technique as a form of treatment for physical, emotional, or medical
problems without the advice of a physician, either directly or indirectly. The
intent of the author is only to offer information of a general nature to help
you in your quest for emotional and spiritual well-being. In the event you use
any of the information in this book for yourself, which is your constitutional
right, the author and the publisher assume no responsibility for your actions.

Any people depicted in stock imagery provided by Thinkstock are
models, and such images are being used for illustrative purposes only.
Certain stock imagery © Thinkstock.

Printed in the United States of America.

ISBN: 978-1-4525-9484-2 (sc)
ISBN: 978-1-4525-9485-9 (e)

Library of Congress Control Number: 2014905347

Balboa Press rev. date: 04/08/2014

THE GENTLE PERSUASION OF CLAUDIA MARDEL

A foreword to *Where The Desert Meets The Cedar*
by Maria Barnas

> Those of us who lingered in the world, seduced by the annunciation of wonderful events, went through life with beautiful and fateful eyes, carrying within us the music of a lovely and tragic mythology. Our mouths utter obscure prophecies. Our minds are invaded by images of the future. We are the strange ones, with half of our beings always in the spirit world.
>
> – Ben Okri, from the novel *The Famished Road*.

She saw me wince. 'Did that hurt?' she asked.

I nodded as she stuck the needle deeper in my ear.

'OUCH!' I exclaimed, getting a little worried, as I suddenly saw the predicament I was in. There were acupuncture needles stuck in my flesh, from my toes to my head. A single movement would cause the needles to move in unwelcome places. It would be impossible for me to flee. The daunting of this truth made me want to run as fast as I could.

Instead I succumbed to the whiff of incense that wafted over me.

It was the first time I ever underwent treatment like this. If not for the gentle persuasion of Claudia Mardel, the author of this book, I would have never let anyone stick needles in my body voluntarily.

I experienced a deep rest, but also felt areas in my body heat up, as if they were telling me to pay closer attention to them. One area in my ear particularly hurt when Mardel stuck a needle in it. I considered not saying anything, as I didn't want to seem unthankful for her treatment.

Claudia held my throbbing ear and said with the solemnity of a surgeon:' Your archway to the spiritual world is blocked.'

I was deeply shocked. Maybe it wasn't just the spiritual world that refused to show itself to me in any way, maybe it was *me* blocking contact with other worlds than my immediate surrounding. Maybe it was my ear.

'Can you open it?' I asked Claudia. Surely the surge of pain in my ear should be enough sacrifice for the spiritual world?

Claudia shrugged her shoulders.

I think she didn't want to disappoint me.

'Just rest', she said.

⟡

With a firmly closed archway to the spiritual world in my ear, what Claudia Mardel made visible for me was the possibility of at least envisioning another world, even though, as to this day, I haven't found a way in.

Mardel's conviction and gentle persuasion, combined with a thorough understanding for those who are less gifted in receiving other-worldly signs, make *Where The Desert Meets The Cedar* such a great read.

The voice in this tale of exploration is highly individual, strong and always open for the unexpected. It takes the reader along an amazing route of inner conflicts, and a struggle in the outer world, a route that is determined by a strong belief in the power of personal growth.

Strangely, a lot of drama lies in what the story does not mention. A lot of questions the reader will ask himself while reading this story, remain unanswered. Where is the family the narrator left behind in Germany? What did the husband she left behind in Maui, exactly look like? What happens to the animals and individuals the narrator meets on her way?

Convention in literature has told me to expect all kinds of details for me as a reader to be filled in. Claudia Mardel, the author of *Where The Desert Meets The Cedar* had no interest in convention, neither in her life, nor in her style of writing.

The main message in this tale, that is based on her own life, is that it is possible to choose your own destiny, with respect for what nature has installed in you as a gift.

The open attitude of Mardel towards the world can be daunting for the reader who expects conformation in his old ways.

Mardel encourages us to open our eyes, to properly look at ourselves and take the necessary action. The spiritual world is a natural world for Mardel, and anyone who is new to the idea that spirits may be guiding most of our quests and attempts in life, will look at their own world in a new light.

WHERE THE
DESERT MEETS
THE CEDAR

CONTENTS

TRANSITION INTO
ANOTHER WORLD

 ∼⌒∽

At no time was I by myself after Shambu passed away. At the moment of death of a loved one, God comes very close, transcending time and space, making only the important things clear, creating synchronicity.

When I got the call from our friend that he had found Shambu dead in our Yurt, I knew this before he spoke. All day long I had felt Shambu working on me and not known why. Now it became clear. He was preparing me for the news I would receive that evening. It was subtle energy work, and I felt that he moved a tremendous amount of energy throughout the day. I felt his hands on me like I had when he did Polarity, Craniosacral, or any magical therapy on me.

When I heard our friend's voice telling me that he had found my husband on the couch, acupuncture needles next to him, likely having experienced a heart attack, my mind did not for one split second doubt the unbelievable information he shared with me. I broke down crying. I got out of the car and just sat there for a long time at the gas station on my way back from Cochiti until someone helped me back into the car. My mind started organizing flights back to Maui. I knew exactly what I needed to do, what I needed to pack, what to take and not to take, how long to stay. There were absolutely no questions in my mind. There was only clarity. This state lasted for a long time, certainly for the 17 days I was on the island, and even for a long time after that. Some remains with me to this day.

What also happened was that I could tell by looking at people's faces when they would die, not by the exact day, but I knew who would die soon. I first noticed this while observing people in the airport and later received confirmation from others. Over the next weeks and months I would call people whose relatives had passed away the day before or just hours before. I started to have a very real and true connection with the other world. It has become another gift. I have always been able to read the color of people's faces and tell if they had cancer or other illness, but this was another level of insight.

When I got to Maui, a friend met me at the airport and took me to the hospital, where I was supposed to take care of some things. I had to wait a couple of days for the autopsy results. My friend took me home. She dropped me off at the gate, and I told her I would just leave my bags there and pick them up later. I wanted to walk down the path of the 80 acres we had taken care of for many years. I started walking, and every root, every rock, every smell and sound was so familiar. The sun was getting lower, and it was still hot from the August heat. Halfway down the road I saw the ATV with the key in it. I don't know why it had been left there or who left it there, but it was perfect. It had a little trouble starting but it did start for me. It was one of those magical things—I asked it to start, it did, and I drove back to pick up my bags. I could not imagine that I would want to leave again that night.

I drove further down into the forest and saw my car parked and covered, as it was not working. The last conversation I'd had with my husband was about the car. I passed it, and the dogs were barking. I called my dog, Kekua, as he was the only one who knew me. The other dogs did not. I had been gone for almost a year, and Shambu had gotten these two new puppies. When they saw that Kekua was endlessly happy to see me, they trusted me and came close. I could tell they had been through a lot of trauma and needed gentleness and healing just as much as I did. Kekua was relieved to see me and knew that things would be okay now. The dogs had been with my husband for almost two days before he was found. I had been trying to call Shambu and it was unusual that he would not call me back, but then again, he had asked for more space. When he did not show up at the office, they looked for him.

I went into the Yurt, put down my bags, and sat down, sobbing. Time stopped. My heart was so incredibly heavy, as if someone had torn it open with huge force. There it was inside out, raw, and unprotected. I cried and cried and cried. I sat in the hammock outside, listening to the wind and the birds. It was getting dark. One of the dogs,

3

Sita, cried also and would only stop when I held her in my arms. So I tried to sleep in bed but, I couldn't because the dog cried so hard it was even more heart breaking. I had lit incenses and candles. There was some Frankincense someone had left. I slept on the floor with the dogs in my arms, or I should say rested, as I could not sleep.

I had a very clear picture of these two black dogs, Sita and Radhe, being the guardians to the underworld. They were like sphinxes standing left and right to lead and guard Shambu. The pictures I saw were amazing and also what Shambu explained to me from the other side. It was about why he had left, and how much he loved me; he gave me glimpses of the other side. Conversations came back to me that we had had days and weeks before. He had told me that he was going to leave this earth, but my mind just could not conceive of it. He had asked me if I could keep our married name, Mardel. It was important to him. He said there weren't any Mardels around anymore. He had told me that he had left my name on the business account, so that I could shift things around. He had asked me if I could finish his life work if he could not do it, and I promised him that I would. All this happened in different conversations, and there were more even subtler things he had said. But for some reason I could not see it. I had just booked a flight back to Maui to see him in September. When I told him, he had said: "Oh, that would be something—to see you again." He knew he would not see me again.

I felt tremendous guilt at not having returned sooner, for having left Maui, for not having made things happen, for leaving him, for every mistake I had made in our relationship. I was incredibly sad, but the guilt was a huge burden on my shoulders. It was still dark when I got up. I was in a different time zone, bright and awake. I turned on the computer and iPad to see if I could get into any of his email accounts to let people know about his passing. Instead, the iPad was playing some music. It was the Beatles singing "All You Need Is Love," just this one song, over and over again. I did not know how to turn it off. It was way too early to call anybody to ask how, and I had no interest in researching how to turn off an iPad. I put a pillow over it and tried to tune it out. But getting into any accounts was easy. My mind was given the passwords, combinations of numbers, and so forth. It was astounding!

I responded to people he had just emailed. I tried to find numbers I would need once it got light enough to call people. I could not find numbers for any of his family, like his sister or brother. I started making calls. One of my Hawaiian friends, Auntie Nani, asked immediately who was with me and said she would come out, she would be there within 20 minutes. I knew Auntie Nani lived on the other side of the island and it was impossible for her to get there this quickly; it would take her at least 1 ½ hours. But she called friends, and they arrived in 20 minutes. From that moment on, I was no longer alone unless I wanted to be. Someone was always with me. The Maui family is incredibly tight and strong that way. It was unbelievable. I don't know how I can ever thank everyone for what they did for me and us in those days. My heart is still overflowing with gratitude toward each person who brought me food, brought me their stories, their teachings, their blessings, their honest feelings of compassion, their own sadness and grief, their condolences. So many people helped to dissolve the household and everything that came with it. Mahalo nui loa.

I don't know how I could have organized everything and dissolved a whole household and clinic, find homes for the animals who would stay on Maui, organize shipping for the ones I would take, get health certificates, talk with the hospital, the mortuary, the airlines, the banks, cancel credit cards, and have a memorial. It was not just the loss that seemed unbearable, but the number of details. My friend offered to take me to the mortuary to explain who Shambu was. We did not want him to be merely a number; we wanted them to know what an amazing healer, mentor, and teacher he was. My friend Kealohikina had made me a healthy energy smoothie with lots of love, and we "talked story" as we drove to Wailuku. She gave me some beautiful advice only a Kapuna can give. She listened and understood. She understood why I had to leave and why things went the way they did. It was amazing to be able to spend time with her.

Every time I needed some help there was just the right person to help me along. Just when I thought I would break down and I would just go where Shambu already was, someone came along and helped me up again. I felt Shambu right there with me at every step. He still is, to this day.

With the guilt came anger now that I was looking at

the storage container that I had asked him for years to deal with. It was back on me to deal with all this stuff! I had to go through boxes and boxes of things, some hardly used, some precious things, some to throw away, some to keep. I wanted to ship one container later. Most of the things I gave away. I gave away so much, clothes, furniture, books, tapes, cars, flashlights, on and on. I got angry because he took the easy way out, he just left all this stuff and left. I was so angry. Why had he not taken me with him!? I was angry about that. He had told me though before he died, that he had already left once and had taken me. He had to come all the way back because he realized it was not my time and I still had things to do here. I still cannot quite believe that even when he made this statement, I did not comprehend that he was going to die.

I prepared and packed boxes at night, so people could keep helping me during the day. I ate very little. During the day, I organized things I could not do at night. I got very little sleep and honestly I don't know where I got the energy to do all the things I did or how I kept up with it for so long. It took me out of the helpless zone, the zone where I would have to feel. Yet, I did feel. The day came when we had a memorial at the beach. I totally did not feel ready or prepared. I remember the beautiful memories and songs people shared. Shambu had been on the island for so many years and was part of so many religious circles. He would never throw out a religion but rather added them to the collection he already practiced. So there were many prayers going on for him all over the world.

The ashes were prayed over by the lama before I would spread them. It was completely clear to me where this was going to be. Kipahulu. Hale Mano. That is where Shambu had first landed on the island, and that is where we got married. A small circle of friends gathered, and my Hawaiian friend did the ceremony. It was beautiful. I asked Uliai if she would come with me to spread the ashes into the ocean. We walked down the path and did our own blessings before I spread the ashes into the ocean. I stood on a cliff from which I could not reach the ocean. Then I realized I could not recycle part of Shambu; I had to rinse the plastic bag. So I stepped onto another rock further down, realizing that the rock I had been standing on was a huge turtle shaped rock. Hanu. I still could not reach the ocean. I took my clothes off and hesitated—it was still quite a way to jump in. Then, a wave came way up to the level of the rock, picked me up ever so gently and took me out into the ocean. It was totally Shambu playing with me! I played with the waves and said my last good-byes. It was a magical experience to be so close to someone who had just left this earth and to be connected in spirit. Nothing mattered, nothing was hurting, nothing was angry or sad. I was just ONE with him and the universe. I will always remember this experience, this feeling. People can tell you these words but to really understand it, you have to experience it.

The weeks and months that followed were filled with organizing things, buying a house where I could keep all of my animals, shipping the rest of the things from the island to New Mexico, and taking care of paperwork. It is amazing how much paperwork there is. I slowly started my grieving process without being busy with things. For months I would lie in my bed and cry at night, sobbing, feeling the pain in my heart. I thought that if I embraced the sadness I would come out on the other side. I did not. I cried and thought every night, there could not possibly be any more tears but there were. It was very draining, so I made the decision to close my heart, so I could start working again and living my life. But little incidences like receiving a check for an insurance case my husband had done months ago, or coming across something on the computer that caught me by surprise, mostly things that were unexpected, would throw me back into tears and I knew I still had a long way to go.

Almost a year had passed when suddenly my beloved dog, Kalima, my partner of 12 years, was dying. His health declined rapidly, and once again I stopped my life to be with him and assist in his dying process. Again my friends here helped me. I did not feel I had the right to take Kalima's life. I asked an animal communicator who had helped me many times to help me communicate with Kalima about this decision. Kalima was so unconscious that he only showed her the dreams he had of Maui. So I told him that I would take care of him but that it was o.k. to let go, and that I knew Shambu was waiting for him on the other side. In that moment Shambu stepped into the conversation, and the animal communicator told me these were two "nevers", an animal showing his dream and someone stepping into the conversation from the other side. Shambu said that in fact, he was waiting for Kalima on the other side with open arms and that Kalima could choose any age he wanted to be, as every day was a good day. Apparently you choose the age for your body over there! Shambu also conveyed the message that he was still waiting for me to write the book that his dad had started and we had worked on for years.

So once again I had friends helping after a few days I spent with Kalima, lying in his dog bed and just holding him; this was his request for comfort. During these days, as I was partially dying with Kalima, I went to other, very beautiful worlds with him. Once again, I did not want to come back. Very slowly I realized that Shambu was always there, he would teach me things, and I would hear his voice if I just listened. He would come to me in my dreams and teach, but also during the day I would hear his words. He told me about the book and that I needed to start over. He realized it was so much bigger, now that he was on the other side. He told me he would not ask me to do something if he knew I could not do it and to trust that he would get the information to me.

My friends took Kalima and me to my trusted vet in Santa Fe, as I no longer could function well. It was hard to now lose my other best friend. I had no agenda of keeping him, I had promised him I would always take care of him and I did. I never was upset with him. Our love was unconditional. We trusted and knew each other. There were no hidden thoughts, no being upset about anything, just pure love. In this state I healed some of what I had been unable to do for Shambu when he left so suddenly. The vet came to the car where I held my dog in my arms, my hand on his heart. When his heart had stopped I slowly got out of the car and just threw myself on the ground crying. I felt Shambu's hand on the back of my heart, touching me ever so gently and I heard his words "Let me take over from here; you have done your part," and he took Kalima's spirit. He was not just waiting on the other side, but rather came all the way down to pick up Kalima. He never had to go through this journey alone. I stopped crying and felt nothing but peace.

Realizing that someone you loved is this close but not still living in the physical body, yet still giving advice and teachings is wonderful. It becomes a different reality. Of course, this would be easier if you established this sort of connection when the person was still alive. I do believe it is possible also if you did not have this type of connection before the other person moved on into another realm. I do want to encourage you to look for this type of connection if you feel inspired by my story.

I realized what I had been through and how much I had suffered, but that I was still alive. I had somehow managed to keep my life going with work and responsibility for all my animals, a mortgage, building a new life, finding new friends, and everything that comes with moving to a new place. I had grown and stretched in so many directions and levels. I had gone through the dark night of the soul, turned over every corner and crevice of my heart, and found what needed to be discarded, what needed to be cherished, and what needed to be replaced with new programs.

Most of all I found myself in the process. I discovered

who I was and what I was about. There was no losing myself in the other, the partner – it was just me, and I found myself on so many levels. I found things I liked and things I needed to change. I knew that I was a person with depth, but I did not previously know how deep this depth was. I discovered the uncomfortable places, my fears, what I had neglected, and what I needed to catch up on. I apologized to people whom I thought deserved an apology if I had done them wrong. I can honestly say there is not a person in the world with whom I am not pono, good. I started really loving myself, being comfortable with myself, starting a real relationship with myself. I started to like to hang out with myself.

I realized that in this deep grief of mine I wish I could have done things differently with Shambu, with my relationship with him. I started treating each person as if it could be the last time I saw him or her. I no longer held back in giving a hug when I felt like it or saying, "I love you," out of fear they might think I was weird. I told people what I thought, in a nice way, of course, but I had earned my right to speak the truth. I no longer care so much what others think. I have held back all of my life to show how sensitive I was and how misunderstood I felt. I knew that most people could not totally relate to me and my over-sensitivity, as some call it, and it no longer mattered. I am speaking my truth. I am authentic, raw, open, vulnerable, and strong. There is nothing you can tell me about myself that I haven't looked at and found peace with, even the things I do not like or did not like.

I have come to know God, or whatever you want to

call the presence that is all around us, very intimately. I have come to know this feeling of being ONE with at the depth of my soul. I never was afraid of dying really. I had asked this question when I was three years old. What happens when we die? And my whole life revolved around this question and led me to study religions and teachings, not just in scriptures, but by traveling and sitting in meditation on this subject over many months. It was the suffering I could not come to terms with. There had to be a way to eliminate it or at least make it more comfortable. What an attachment! I learned to let go of attachments and expectations, and there are always more levels of the letting go process.

I have become a woman, a soul with wisdom, an elder in some way as young as I am. I have always been able to help people with my words and advice, but all these experiences have led me to yet another depth. I now have tools to pass on, because I had to find tools to help myself. Life is beautiful. Life is perfect. Life is indescribable.

JUMPING OFF THE CLIFF— LEAVING GERMANY

T he first time you jump is the scariest, isn't it? Once you have jumped a couple of times it becomes easier. When I look back on my life, I have taken a lot of jumps and leaps. The first was when I left Germany. I was 25 and living in Berlin. I liked Berlin and the people. They had a great sense of humor, but I realized that I was not a city girl. My dog and I would find a park for many hours every day to get "out of the city". At the time, I was in an unfulfilling relationship, having married too young and without a clear vision for my life. I was in such a deep depression that I no longer wanted to remain on this earth. Most of the people I met were on a similar journey but did not want to change anything. I knew I had to leave to make change happen.

I went on vacation and fell in love. I left behind my whole life in Germany. I ended the relationship I had there, packed up my belongings, and moved. My new partner, Michael, and I went diving and did a lot of fun things. I felt renewed excitement, freedom, and joy in my life. Life was worth living! One morning Michael got a call that his dad had been flown to Miami on an emergency flight and had been diagnosed with pancreatic cancer. So we dropped everything and set up a place in Miami to take care of Michael's dad and his wife during the nine to ten months of the dying process. Initially, he fought the cancer, thinking he would make it through, but later, he came to accept that he had had an incredible life, and it was okay to let go. I admired the grace and celebration with which this man faced his death. He invited people from all around the world to see him one last time and celebrate life with him. It was an amazing journey! It was not easy for anybody, but we all learned so much in the process. With my German origin, I was not accustomed to people being so open hearted. I got a lot of healing through this journey with Michael and his dad.

After Michael's dad had passed very peacefully, we went traveling the world for years, diving and sailing. At some point we both felt we wanted to put down some roots. Michael had bought a ranch on Maui. I started a Hawaiian plant nursery, learning all about the plants, their history, and what the Hawaiian people would use them for. When I set my mind on doing something, I always give it more than 100%. I had a whole nursery going in no time. I also wanted to continue studying the healing arts and went to massage school. I absolutely loved Maui and the people there. I loved the experiences I had there and knew it was my home. The stock market tanked and Michael incurred huge losses. He wanted to sell the ranch and with it, my dream. I was heart-broken. I could not understand how he could not share my vision about a ranch where we could have therapeutic riding, healing through planting, learning about health, doing massage and acupuncture, and make this happen. Forget the stock market!

Our relationship fell apart. Because I had gone in and out of the country many times, and was now on a student visa living in the U.S. I had a very limited time to figure this out! I was lying on the massage table of one of my massage teachers, Shari, whom I loved dearly. I entered a deep space and could hear gongs and Buddhist chants. I shared this experience with her. She told me that she had wanted to go to China, Nepal and India to learn about acupuncture and attend the Kalachakra Initiation in India, but her partner had just cancelled the trip. Would I like to come? Well, there was no question in my mind. That was just what I needed to figure out what I was going to do. I went home and prepared for the trip that was coming up rather quickly.

JUMPING OFF THE CLIFF—SEARCHING FOR NEW HORIZONS

~

We traveled to China first and found that there weren't really any acupuncturists left; they all had to leave the country. China must have been beautiful at some point, but I experienced it as grey—the country, the land, and the people. I was glad to leave and enter an amazing place, rich in history, culture and religious practice—Nepal. Did I love Kathmandu and the smells of incenses around every corner, hearing the chants almost all day and night, seeing prayer wheels spinning and people dedicating their whole lives in this way to pray for peace and freedom! It had to be one of the clearest spaces I have experienced in terms of energy and high altitude air, with people praying and focusing on the higher good of humanity all day long. We spent a couple of days in the countryside before we went to our main destination: India.

I had been to India before and did not like it at all. I had grown in many ways since then and understood the culture better. I was there for spiritual reasons rather than sightseeing this time. We found our little family-run domicile and looked into all the meditation practices and initiations that we could attend before the actual Kalachakra Initiation. I took refuge with the Buddhists and when the Venerable K.C. Ayang Rimpoche gave me my Buddhist name, Phema Kandro which he translated as Dakini of the Lotus, I pondered it for a very long time. It felt like there was a mission to it. Then I began to sit for weeks in meditation doing Phowa, learning about death and dying, meditating and saying mantras, getting to know Buddha Amithaba intimately! Phowa is all about transferring consciousness at the time of death and getting the initiation to do so.

After this we had some time to do bodywork and integrate all we had just meditated on and learned! Then it was time for the Kalachakra Initiation and Empowerment, which were given by H.H. Karmapa and H.H. Dalai Lama together. What an amazing thing to experience! The Kalachakra is a tantric practice relating to cycles of time. There are three such cycles, each of which is analogous to the other two: first the external cycles of time, through which the universe passes, secondly the internal cycles, through which the body passes, and thirdly the alternative cycles, referring to the Kalachakra empowerment and practice, and to enlightenment.

The sand painting the monks had created was just amazing, and so was the experience of this initiation and empowerment practice. Many times I found myself sitting down for meditation, thinking only a few minutes had elapsed, when in our timeline hours had passed! The experience and transmissions are indescribable. The magic and experiences I had in India and the memories of past lives could be a whole other book!

It was time to return to Maui, and at the airport I literally collapsed. I thought I was dying right there out of fear of what I would have to go through when I got home. This collapsing because of fear would happen to me a few times more in different situations, and I really got to know how it came on and how I could work with it. I knew I had to end my relationship and start another life. I knew I had only so much time before having to face moving back to Germany or finding another country with quarantine laws like Hawaii's, so I could later ship my dog back to Maui. I felt so overwhelmed that I could only thank my teacher, Shari, that I actually made it back home.

I had taken a break from massage school and had to wait until the next class was where I had left off, but it had been so worth the three-month journey. It completely changed my life. All of a sudden, so many synchronistic things started happening. The Kalachakra continued for months after it was completed in India. First I tried to ignore that my relationship was no longer working and what I had figured out in India sitting in meditation for so long. At some point I could no longer do this and started to develop a plan. Massage school had started again, and I met some very nice people in my new class. I had moved out and stayed with a friend for some time. Next, I rented a place, often spending nights at the beach when that situation did not work.

One day my beloved dog, Kalima, got poisoned and I rushed him to the vet. Placing him in the back of my truck, leaving the ranch where I had lived for years with Michael and still taking care of my nursery there, I realized it was not just my dog who was dying but also myself! I drove way too fast while on the phone with the vet, telling him exactly what my dog needed, from oxygen to drugs. My higher consciousness had taken over, giving me exactly what I needed the vet to prepare to save my dog's life! I got there not one minute too early, everything was ready, and we just hooked him up to the oxygen with one collapsed lung, the other one threatening to collapse. We got blood tests, x-rays, IVs, and on and on. Hours later, the vet told me that he did not know if he could save my dog and I should come in to see him. I did. There he was on the vet table. He was still so young, not even two! I loved Kalima. I told Kalima that I would not give up and would not let the vet give up and to just hang in there. The vet talked about costs and I told him I did not care about costs, please just save my dog! I gave him my credit card. What a bizarre situation! There was no time to get angry. Finally after many hours Kalima started breathing by himself. Ironically the oxygen machine was now dead, it stopped working as soon as Kalima started breathing by himself. Kalima breathed the life out of it.

The vet kept my dog for the first night, which I would not have allowed had I anymore strength left in me, but I needed rest. I knew we were not over it yet. And I would have to be strong for weeks taking care of my beloved Kalima. I knew I had to find a place to live. I could not have Kalima living at the beach in this condition. My dear friend, Steve, to whom I will be forever grateful, took a stance against his landlord who did not allow dogs and took both of us in. I slept with Kalima in my arms so I could feel it if he moved with the drip going. We lay on the deck, and I sang to him for hours, telling him that if he really no longer wanted to be around, I would let him go; if he decided to stay with me, I would take care of him the best I could, forever. Slowly we started to go for tiny walks with the drip still going. We followed a special diet. Kalima became stronger and healthier. After some weeks, we had to look for a place of our own. The place we found wasn't ideal but it would work.

This episode opened my eyes to the importance of caring for myself. By not listening with clarity to what I had received about my relationship not working, I had allowed all these energies, disturbances and poisons to enter my field. My dog had taken it all on for me, like dogs do, and he almost gave his life for it! I would learn from it and do better. I promised myself this, giving thanks that Kalima was still with me.

Another friend showed up in my life and helped me along. Donny. Bless his heart! He came by and picked me up to help me find a car one afternoon, as I had to return my truck. He drove around in an old beat-up Jeep, not because he could not afford anything else but because he liked to fit into the local scene. He lived in Kaanapali, the Westside of Maui and would strap his surfboard to the Jeep and go surfing a lot. We drove around and he pointed to a silver Bronco at the Ford dealer's parking lot.

He said: "that is your new car". I smiled. I liked the car. It had red seats and windows all around, four-wheel drive, and I would be able to go anywhere in it. I would even be able to sleep in the back of it with Kalima if I had to. We checked it out, I bought it, and we named it Silverfox. Donny put me on his insurance since I could not get an insurance policy at the time. For the next few weeks and months I drove to see Donny on the other side of the island whenever I needed a break. He was so helpful and generous with his advice, and he always made me laugh. We had great times together! He would have me stand at the beach facing the breaking waves and teach me the pirate laugh. It is a laugh that comes deep from the belly and it has to come out loud and confident and instills courage. I practiced. It made me feel better! It made me feel courageous. Donny was in my close circle of friends for years until he passed away at way too young an age.

When I got the news I was so sad and I could not believe it. Donny had told my husband at the time that he thought he would not be around for very much longer. He did not want to scare me so I did not know about it until afterwards. Donny had put everything in order, cleaned his office, and organized everything so he was able to leave the planet. What an amazing inspirational teacher he was to me and to so many other people. To me he was a bodhisattva who had done so many good things on this planet that God had called him; his life work was done on this earth. At his memorial so many of his friends and coworkers shared stories similar to the ways in which I had experienced Donny. He wanted his memorial to be a celebration, but I could not keep myself from crying and crying for the loss I felt. I knew he was not afraid to die. I remembered the tattoo that he had gotten in Tahiti from a tribal member who had talked about the crossing of the big ocean and new adventures in a far away land. I remember the tattoo from giving Donny a massage when he had just gotten the tattoo on his trip to Tahiti. He had invited me to come on the trip, but I was too scared about being unable to return to this country. Donny's memorial was an honorary one; it was a celebration for the warrior he truly was! His ashes were taken out to sea on a canoe and spread to the wind. Kahunas and Hawaiian elders performed the celebration, and his friends went out on their surfboards to guide Donny one last time. This was the spot Donny had worked close by and surfed in the morning at sunrise or enjoyed the sunset on the ocean. The waves were calm. Once Donny was released to the wind, a set of waves kissed the beach and the people at the shore so gently – Donny saying A hui ho – Until we meet again – one more time. It was a beautiful Farewell. I missed Donny, and it hurt my heart that he was gone, but I have fond memories of him. I will always remember his huge bear hug and his laugh. I have warmth in my heart thinking of Donny. Even today I sometimes have conversations with him and know exactly which advice Donny would give me in a situation. He is always there when I need him!

THE NEW HORIZON

❧

I was almost finished with massage school and I had to figure out what to do next. I was trying to find homes for my plants, which I still watered every day, while thinking about letting things go and possibly moving to a different country. I did not really want to go back to Germany. I thought New Zealand or Australia might be an option but I would have the same visa issues. At least I could take my dog and not have the quarantine issues on my way back to Maui if I could make it back some day.

I had met Shambu some time ago, and at this time we reconnected. I planted some plants for his Acupuncture Center. He had just acquired the lease to a very beautiful building with a garden in the front and back. He was planning to rent rooms to therapists and to do acupuncture himself. We shared time together and started falling in love. It was a very beautiful time. We went out to Kipahulu together to his friend's land, where he had landed when he came to Maui many years ago. We went to a celebration for Auntie Helen's memorial and took time on our way back, enjoying drinking from coconuts, lying on the beach, and hanging out under the trees in the shade. He taught me so much. He taught me how to manifest things, how to set my intention, how to attract things. He wanted to help me to help myself. That I find is one of the greatest gifts someone can give you because you can always help yourself even if no one is around. We played on so many levels, we had prayers. It was a magical time.

I was present when Auntie Diane blessed the Acupuncture Center and the people who would be involved in it. She was a kind woman with a sharp, clear mind and lots of mana, as the Hawaiians say – power. She walked around with Tileaves and salt water in a bowl made out of Koa wood. She had a Bible with her and cleared the space. Over the following weeks, Shambu and I drove around finding the most beautiful Tileaves, planting them all around the house for protection. He had a prayer with me and for me to be able to stay in the country. I was thankful to have found someone who helped. I moved in with Shambu and finished massage school. I helped him set up his Acupuncture Center. Other friends, Sumner and Angi, offered to keep my plants at their place, because I had to remove them from their present location. With the help of my friend Anna and her husband, Don, I moved every plant. Sumner and Angi would eventually plant all the plants around their house and take care of them. I was so thankful! All of my plants had a home. The seeds and nurturing had not been wasted. I was happy. It had been quite the move, and there were a lot of plants! My friends had pulled together. In retrospect, I see that friends have always showed up in time. I have put out a lot of energy to help others in different situations, and I believe that help is returned. While it might not be reciprocated by the same person, Universe provides the best qualified people for the current task. I have learned to accept help, because this is what friends are for. I never take anything for granted, appreciating all who have helped in my journey. When someone needs help I don't hesitate to do the same. I believe that our purpose is to make life easier and more enjoyable for each other.

JUMPING OFF THE CLIFF INTO MARRIAGE!

S hambu asked me to marry him. We both knew we had been together for only a short time and that we were taking a risk. He wanted me to stay in the country, and we did honestly love and respect each other. I was overjoyed. He said that he would marry me solely to keep me in the United States, but it was not the reason for his proposal. It was because we loved each other. We were married within weeks. It came together beautifully and simply. Friends appeared to help. We were married on the land out in Kipahulu, where Shambu had first arrived on Maui. Nala created the most beautiful heart-shaped cake covered with red and pink Impatiens flowers. My friend Dominique showed up to wish me well, and my friend, Steve, had picked up doves whom we set free for our celebration. Uliai had given me her most beautiful pendant and had made sure the esthetics of her place were beautiful, reflecting love, joy, and beauty. We had a fire and sang songs; we had the drum and rattle; our friends joined the celebration. The people who were supposed to be present were there, despite a hard rain that closed the road to Hana. As usual, though, it was as it was supposed to be, and it was perfect. Shambu and I spent a few days in one of the Yurts on the land. I said I would like to live in a Yurt. The round shape and the canvas between the single room and the outside world gave me a beautiful feeling. I could feel the elements and trees around me. I enjoyed this close connection with nature, hearing every sound of the birds and the waves. For us, this was a time filled with magic and bliss. I was the happiest woman in the world! Slowly my worries fell away. It took some time to become accustomed to not having to worry.

We lived in Haiku at the time. The ocean was close, and it was not far to Paia the home of our Acupuncture Center. I graduated from massage school and took the Hawaii licensing exam, which finally enabled me to work. It was fun. Slowly, we built our home and our Center. We worked very hard while still having fun planting the garden and helping it flourish. Gradually, other therapists joined us.

We started looking for land where we might be able to put up a Yurt. We had so much fun exploring the island, going to remote, off-the-beaten track places. One day a client overheard us talking about the land we were trying to find. He told us he had a piece of land for which he would love to find a caretaker. There was nothing on it, but we could look. I was so excited! I loved the area he was talking about; it was not far from where I had lived on the 22-acre ranch. We closed the office for the day and went to see the land. Because it was summer, the land was dry. I had seen this part of the island turn from dry to green with an inch or two of rain. There was nothing green now, and the Wiliwili trees were leafless. I immediately loved the land. It was peaceful, still, and surrounded on three sides by two ranches with cattle. On the upper part, a road led to a Meditation Center and the homes of a few neighbors. This large piece of land was special; it was handed down for generations and had had only one owner before this one. It was surrounded by rock walls and had lots of rock wall structures on it. I knew I wanted to live there. How could we make this happen? It was different from Haiku and farther from Paia and from the ocean. I knew Shambu was used to being close to the ocean and being surrounded by lush greenery. But he liked the land and saw how excited I was.

So we talked to the man who had just offered us living space on the land. He agreed to our putting up a Yurt and living in the forest. Shambu and I began looking for the location. I spent more time out there with my friend, Anna, because I was so happy and excited about all the Native Hawaiian trees that had survived on this land and had not been overgrazed by cattle. I wanted to start as soon as possible. I took my dowsing rods out to locate the ideal spot, safe from weather and close to any water. My dowsing rods lead me to the perfect place, nestled among the grown trees, surrounded by a rock formation to shelter it from winds and storms. There were rock walls below us. The road was drivable but rough. We would have to carry water and other necessities, which would be quite a chore. We also needed to be out of sight, because a Yurt might not meet code requirements. In addition, not knowing the future of the land, we thought it best to be tucked away in a corner at the end of the road. So I marked the spot I had just dowsed and showed it to Shambu. He liked it. Our landlord approved. We began to work on the project. We hired help. Some of our friends were happy to have work. We started building a platform, we put the Yurt up, we put on the roof with the help of experienced friends. We had a prayer, sang songs, and spent our first night there. The dog house was the place for a coffee pot, and we had our first hot brewed coffee in the morning. We still needed to get water lines. We were living out of 5 gallon containers filled at the Acupuncture Center, where we also took showers and did laundry. We had moved our carpets and furniture in. It felt great to be between the trees, and I loved hearing the deer and the owls at night. During our second night, there was a huge Kona storm.These storms come from the South, bringing lots of water. We had water inside the Yurt. The roof was not on quite straight. Well, at least we could figure it out before winter. We took the wet carpets out, which sounds easier than it was. Those carpets were heavy! We needed help in straightening the roof because of the heavy liner and underlying insulation that needed to remain in place.

Now everything grew and became green overnight! When people told me that they could see the grass grow it was hard to believe, but in Hawaii you actually can. It is amazing how fast the grass grows, how the first shoots come out, and how the rest of the blades become a light green and then darker and more lush with each passing hour. The soil is incredibly good on the islands, missing only calcium, but otherwise, just needing water. In other parts of the island, though, the soil has been destroyed by sugar cane fields and pineapples. It will take a long time before anything organic and healthy can be grown. On our land, though, the soil and the trees were healthy. It was undisturbed, and I felt the presence of nature spirits. We put up wind chimes and crystals, because the fairies like that. They come to tinkling sounds, and they like quiet and peace. We wanted to protect this place. So again Shambu planted Tileaves. We cut a lot of the glycine, a vine that smothers everything with its weight and deprives growing plants of light. We worked a lot! If we did not work in the Acupuncture Center, we worked at home, building an outdoor kitchen, shower, and bathroom within the lava rocks. We lived very simply, and sometimes it was difficult to keep things clean.

THE FAMILY

When we lived in Haiku Kalima was our only dog. He had a friend, Lakshmi, a cat whom I had brought home one day while we were living at our old place. I had just parked and gone into a store. Looking back out through the entry, I saw a big red truck pull out of it's parking place. A tiny kitten who had been on the front left tire had rolled off and was injured by the turning tire. I witnessed the entire accident and ran outside. The cat was turning in circles, obviously injured and disoriented. I could not get there quickly enough and called for a bystander to pick up the cat. Someone handed me the cat, who was bleeding and had lost part of her ear. I held her close to my chest and rolled up my t-shirt to make her feel safe. I went to my car without doing the shopping and held her on my lap. I had called Shambu to tell him I was bringing home an injured cat. The kitten was so scared that she crawled under my seat. So I got out of the car and needed help to get her out without losing her. I opened the door with Shambu on one side and tried to get her. But she jumped the other way, all claws, and escaped, pursued by Kalima, who hated cats. He chased her into the forest. I was so angry at him! That was the last thing I needed. I wanted to help the cat, not chase her into the forest! I did not know if my dog had killed her or if I would ever see her again. I have never yelled at Kalima to this day, but I was too upset to talk with him for nearly three days.

We were sitting in our swinging chair drinking our morning coffee when Kalima came back from his morning stroll, followed by the cat. She decided to love the whole family and jumped onto the swinging chair, rubbing on us as if we had known her forever. Neighbors who told me I was just wasting the cat food put out for her every night, hoping she was still alive, could not believe it! From then on Kalima and Lakshmi were best friends, had the greatest wrestling matches in the living room, and were inseparable.

We had taken the two of them with us to the land. Lakshmi loved it on the land. She had room to roam, and she was free. She was responsible for the mice but preferred to sleep in bed with me, purring me into my dreams. I love that cat! We thought Kalima needed a dog friend. I called my friends at the Ranch to see if they might have Border Collie puppies. Kalima was a Border Collie/Golden Retriever mix and looked like a blond Border Collie. As a matter of fact they had a Border Collie/Kelpi mix the grandparents decided they did not want because he had too much energy. What a wise decision! I went to pick up the dog, Sergio, whom we renamed Kekua. And boy, did he have a lot of energy. He was non-stop, with only an on and an off switch, nothing in between. I don't know how many times he chewed up my shoes or ran off with socks, underwear, or anything else. He knew exactly how to get attention while remaining just beyond reach. He would bark at the car whenever the motor started and run up and down the road. He needed as much exercise as possible to tire him out. He was way too much, even for me. In the beginning he was so food-aggressive that I fed one dog in front of the house and one behind the house. Kalima would not even dare look at his food when Kekua was around. Kalima did teach Kekua a few tricks, though. Sometimes the two of them would take off after deer. Usually Kalima was the one instigating the chase, and Kekua would keep it going. They would be gone up to four days and nights. I was so worried about them, praying they would come back. I don't know how often I had to drive down to Kihei to pick them up. It was only about three miles from our house but required a 45-minute drive, because there were no roads connecting us. I would call the ranches and tell them that my dogs were gone and ask that they watch out for them. One time golf course security called me to ask me if I was missing a dog and I replied I was actually missing two. They said they had them and they also got a deer, did I want the deer? I could not believe it. I thanked them, told them to tie the black dog to a chain he could not bite through and asked that they find someone who could make use of the deer. I retrieved the dogs, both untied but exhausted. That was it. I hated electric collars but did not know how else to train them not to run off. I ordered the collars, and we got the situation under control. We might have lost them once or twice more if they did not wear the collars but they got so much better about staying with us.

My husband asked our landlord if he would mind if we got a horse. He told him that I always had wanted a horse, and this would be the perfect place. Our landlord said yes, and I looked around for horses. I did not see one I really connected with. Years ago, while on a cattle drive, I had fallen in love with Shebrah, the spunky Quarter horse mare I rode. On our first ride I had to pee so urgently that I stopped, found a tree and held the reins. Shebrah just took off and left me there with my pants down. I got myself back together, and one of the cowboys brought Shebrah back to me. They thought I had fallen off, and I was too embarrassed to tell them what had happened. Falling off usually costs the rider a case of beer, so we left it at that. I loved that dark bay mare! Wendell told me then I could take her home. At the time I could not, because we were still traveling, and I had not settled my visa issues. But now I called my friend to ask if he still had Shebrah. He said yes. I asked if he was willing to sell her. He said that since I had seen her, she had had one colt, been bred, and might be in foal. Although I was a very good rider, I knew little about raising a foal or training a young horse. I did not want to buy Shebrah if she was in foal. But the vet check turned out negative. So I had the fencing put in and worked on the pasture. Then Wendell brought Shebrah to my place. He turned his truck and trailer around in a tight area, skillfully backed up through the narrow gate, and parked. There was my girl! She was calm, and I so loved her eyes that showed so much spirit. Wendell rode her down our long driveway bareback; we followed in the car. We saddled her, and I rode her for a little bit. She was fiery, she was willing, and she was the only horse I wanted. We had a connection. So I put her in the pasture after rinsing and feeding her, although the feed in the pasture was plentiful. My friend commented that Shebrah probably thought she had died and gone straight to heaven. My husband said she was a fat horse anyway, and my friend's reply was "grass belly".

JUMPING OFF THE CLIFF
INTO A LIFE WITH HORSES

∽⟨⟩

I was in heaven. My first owned horse. It had been on my Christmas list every year since my childhood, and I could spell pony when I could hardly write. Here she was, this beautiful mare with her dark eyes and refined head, her strong muscular body, and her slight sway back. I sat with her in the pasture for hours talking to her, singing to her, just hanging out with her. I did not really ride her. I wanted to get her used to the change. She was a little moody, and sometimes I was afraid of her. My husband sometimes helped me with her, although he knew nothing about horses. He had a calming presence and effect on anyone who was upset; aikido is what he called it. I brushed Shebrah every day and cared for her. Then my farrier, Uncle Henry, came all the way to our place to shoe her. I knew him because he shod the horses for whom I previously had been a caretaker. Uncle Henry took one look at my mare and said, "That mare is hapai! I looked at him and asked, "What does that mean?" He

said, "She is pregnant." I told him she had just been vet
checked and was supposedly not in foal. He said, "I have
been around horses all my life... and this mare is pregnant.
I have never been wrong with this. She is probably seven
months along." I was a bit in shock and told him, this
could not be. He laughed and went to shoe her. He gave
me advice on this and that and left me rather confused. I
was excited about the possibility of having a foal grow up
in this incredibly beautiful place. I started taking Shebrah
for short and easy walks and rides to keep her moving.
Every morning before work, I hopped on her and took
the dogs for a walk around the loop with me. It was fun.
I had inquired about the breeding date and prepared a
straw bed at Shebrah's favorite place. Sometimes I got up
in the middle of the night to check on her in the pasture.
I sang and talked with her, sitting on the fallen tree close
to her resting spot.

I checked on Shebrah more frequently as her due
date approached. I got up in the middle of the night to
see her. Although many horses prefer to be alone when
giving birth, some don't mind a human presence. Some
can await a perfect undisturbed time. One morning
Shambu had taken the ATV to take Kekua for a run
and came back saying, "Looks like we got a little deer in
the pasture. You had better go check." I went, and there
they were. Shebrah was standing over her precious little
colt. It could not have been very long since she had given
birth. She looked exhausted but so caring; she was in her
mid teens and had previously had one colt. Although
recently retired from ranch work, she remained strong and

in excellent shape. The little guy was lying on the straw bed I had prepared and was calmly enjoying being in the world rather than squeezed in the belly. Not wanting to disturb their intimacy, I checked on Shebrah and verified that the entire placenta had been delivered. The cute little horse moved his head lying down. He looked adorable, and I was in love. After I spent some time with them, talking with them and looking at them, Shebrah brought her colt to me. He walked over and flopped down in front of me. I petted his back and neck for a little while. Then I became still again. I felt honored that Shebrah had brought him to me. She was very proud of her son. There was no question in my mind about what to name this horse: Kyros. He was born the same day as Kekua had been born a year earlier, August 8. I named him Kyros, after my grandfather's horse whose stories I heard while growing up. My grandfather had taken me riding, nurturing that love and passion in me. I have remained forever grateful for his love and time. It seemed natural to name my little horse after the horse he had loved so much with whom he had shared so many adventures. The little colt had three white socks and one black leg. He had a beautiful white star on his forehead and a little white strip coming up from his left nostril toward the middle of his nose. It was cute, as if he had smoke emanating from his nostril. He was pretty red and not a dark bay like Shebrah. I knew beyond a doubt that this would be a spunky, mischievous fire horse! It was written all over him.

He got up, to nurse and I noticed that his left front leg did not look quite straight. The legs of foals look a little awkward, but this did not seem quite right. Was I imagining things, or was there a problem? The vet arrived the next day to check on Shebrah and her colt. He confirmed that the leg was not quite straight and gave me options for a surgical procedure and time lines. I did not want surgery for my young foal before the growth plates had closed, precluding the possibility of correct bone modeling. Having knowledge about muscle and bone, knowing how much healing is possible with intention, I wanted to try other options before resorting to surgery. My farrier, Uncle Henry, came to check it out and gave me advice, including corrective trimming. The vet had suggested stall rest; my farrier told me let him try his legs out and run around, allowing the opportunity to correct the deformity. I opted for the running around. It seemed not right to confine to a stall a little guy who wanted to explore life, when I had so much pasture. And explore he did! He jumped over logs and went around trees at full speed. He charged Kalima and me, cutting it a little close for my taste at times. We administered treatments to him, including laser, massage, and visualization. We also used acupuncture when he would be still enough. I believe that the spatial awareness he developed while contending with the terrain contributed to healing of his leg. As his chest widened, his leg became straighter. His fetlock compensated somewhat, and to this day he is not perfectly straight. But who is? He travels well, provided that I keep him trimmed for a perfect breakover. The fright I experienced when he was first born caused me to grow as I researched bones, muscles, and treatment options. It made me meditate, visualize, and spend time in a different way with my horses.

I learned a lot from Shebrah this way. In the beginning she had not let me come close without becoming grouchy. I would sit on my fallen tree, waiting and singing to her. Only if I truly was within myself and I had released any wants and needs would she choose to come to me and hang out happily. It took a long time to truly release expectations and simply be. It was so worth it, though! I was able to reach that space more quickly each time I practiced, and today it takes only a moment. I did have to learn it, however. All I wanted then was to swing my arms around her neck to pet her, love her, and touch her. Initially, it was frustrating that she would not allow this. I learned to respect her space and to ask permission to enter the several layers of her space. I could feel her aura from afar and became accustomed to stopping, establishing a connection, and receiving permission before entering that space. In the next layer, several yards from Shebrah, I could feel her cranial pulse. At times, I followed it, explored it, was with it. Even closer to Shebrah, I encountered yet another pulse. Finally I reached her physical body, which I could touch. I did polarity treatments to release energy in her back during her pregnancy. I could feel the foal's energy in her belly. I played my singing bowls for the two of them. Shebrah loved the singing bowls. She still does.

I spent a lot of time at home when Kyros was little. I just loved seeing him run and play. I wanted a connection with him as he grew. All was not as easy, as I knew little about training a horse and never had wanted to raise and train a foal. The Universe makes us learn and grow. I read books, listened to the old-timers, and tried my luck with Kyros. I haltered him without trouble, as he trusted me. The issue was not lack of trust; it was lack of respect. He was all over me and pretty much did what he wanted to do. Being a very gentle soul, I felt sad and mean at the mere thought of being harsh with Kyros in any way. I got help from others, whose training methods I did not like. Some were too harsh, some did not know what they were doing, some vented their anger onto my horse, some seemed to be more talk than action. Finally, I met Sarah, who helped me in just the right way. She was kind and gentle but did not let anything slip by her notice. I learned everything she could teach me. I practiced what she did with Kyros. His newly learned respect improved our relationship. He still was a handful, being a very intelligent horse with a lot of play drive. He had only his mama and me as playmates, there being no other colts or fillies. Much as I wished I could provide him with equine playmates, it was not possible in my life at that time.

Our electric fencing was hot but not hot enough. The gate was next to my tack and grooming shed, and often I would squeeze through the electric fence to get into the pasture. Well, the little guy figured out pretty quickly that he could do the same. Yes, the electric shock was a little annoying but easy enough to endure for a moment to reach the other side. He would then show up in front of the yurt to say good morning. This had become a routine, and Mama Shebrah was not even worried. She knew I would bring him back. Meanwhile, she enjoyed a break from her little enthusiastic colt, who would jump up on her and pee on her hay.

I started riding Shebrah again. I put Kyros in the round pen so he could not escape and would be safe, saddled up Shebrah, and off we went. The first time, she threw a fit! She pinned her ears as we rode out of sight of her colt. She backed up and threatened to ditch me at the steep hill called Donny Pass. My friend Donny had been stuck there, needing rescue from the drop-off. Kyros was whinnying and throwing a fit himself in the round pen. I knew Shebrah could be quite calculating, so thinking better safe than sorry, I gave in. I realized this would set us up for subsequent trouble at this place, and I would need a different approach. I understood her concern at leaving her son alone with no herd to take care of him. I felt compassion for her distress. So we turned around to find Kyros all sweaty and worked up in the round pen. He was so happy to see us. It was fine for him to leave his mama but not the other way around! In that case, I needed a different approach. The next morning, I put Kyros in the round pen again, asked my husband to stay with him, and walked Shebrah. This was better. Initially unwilling to go over Donny Pass, she eventually followed me and, happy that I took my time. Kyros still threw a fit but calmed down with Shambu there. Initially, we left him for only five minutes, gradually increasing the time to ten, fifteen, and then more minutes over several days. It became a routine and less of an issue. Shebrah now let me ride her. Both horses knew what to expect. Then Shebrah started to ask for her morning walks, whinnying and nickering when she heard me coming down the path. She liked when it was just the two of us with the dogs, and she could enjoy herself.

I was happy in my life. I had realized many of my longtime dreams and was enjoying them. I enjoyed being married, having a home, being in the native forest, being with my animals, and experiencing the wild animals and pristine, undisturbed natural surroundings. I was able to dream and write children's stories about fairies, dragons, golden horses, and flooded prairies. I was grateful. I had given up so much and worked so hard. I saw living in the mature native forest as a reward having collected the seeds, planted them, nurtured the grown plants, and found a home for them. The Universe had responded to the care that had come from my heart. The Universe had rewarded my efforts by placing me in this mature forest. I remembered that on one of my excursions to a Reforestation Project I told my friends I would like to live in a Wiliwilitree forest, because those trees are so incredible. They have thorns on their stems and branches, but the wood is light. They respond to the rainy season with the most delicate flowers of red, orange, peach, yellow and a yellow-green shade. Earlier Hawaiians used the trunks for canoes, because it was so light. The tree itself has quite the presence and consciousness, and it is quite a treat to learn from these very protective trees. They are very wise, elderly, precious beings, some of them 80 or 100 years old. At the time, a bug was destroying the trees already weakened by drought. Some had dropped branches or fallen during storms. Our intention was to protect the Wiliwilitree, and it seemed that indeed, they were thriving on our land.

Meanwhile, I was learning a lot about horses. They are highly sensitive emotional beings who can be a bridge between the worlds. They are animals capable of sensing our thoughts and feelings before they reach our conscious awareness. Horses mirror our emotions and help us to heal. Horses do not hold grudges; they forgive. They are grounded, and at the same time they are ethereal beings. We need to become more aware of this and treat horses with the respect they deserve.

I knew it was time to start riding Kyros, who was now three years old. It was not urgent, but I saw the need for help. During my search for help, I participated in a play day with a local Natural Horsemanship group. I met a woman capable of helping me train Kyros. Instead she offered me a job training horses. This was quite the turn of events. I did not have to think about it, as I had watched videos and DVDs while searching for a way to train Kyros in the way I wanted him trained and treated. I immediately committed to the job offered.

A DECISION IS MADE

⟡

The building where we had our Acupuncture Center had been sold, necessitating a restructure of everything. My husband took some time off to write the book about some material his father had passed on to him. I did massage therapy at several locations, until I encountered a situation beyond the scope of what should enter the practice of any massage therapist. I had a client who threatened suicide if I could not help him recover motor use after paralysis. Despite collaboration from physicians, the pressure was beyond my emotional resources. I needed to temporarily distance myself from the massage profession. My personal empathy and compassion overwhelmed the professional training I had received regarding boundaries. This client's pain and suffering were intense beyond what my empathic circuits could process.

I started working for the ranch two miles from my house, enjoying being close to home. I could ride my horse to work, and it was fun taking care of the horses. I took them out on the trails, worked them in the arena or round pen, and eventually started the young ones under saddle. It was quite the journey. I learned and grew stronger as I was doing the physical work required for a ranch job. I learned medical histories and was there for emergencies, aftercare and rehabilitation. I learned in depth, as is my way with any field of study. I enjoy the growth of learning, and I am a fast learner in areas of interest. I applied the new knowledge to my own horses.

Meanwhile, I started training Kyros. We did a lot of groundwork, building a relationship of trust and respect. I walked him and sometimes let him graze. I checked the fence lines with this horse, who was curious and ready for anything. I used a rope halter but no saddle during walks. One day, I found a tree stump and hopped onto his back. Using the rope I led him to the stump, gently swung my leg over his back, and sat on him. Kyros acted as if he had been expecting this turn of events. I used the rope to gently guide Kyros directionally. I squeezed my legs ever so gently and then a little harder. He walked on. I guided him to the dirt road on the property and asked him to walk back home. It went smoothly. I felt so good. He was happy. We did this a few times, and it became a routine. Next, I saddled him in the round pen. The first time, he just lay down on the ground to roll with me on his back. I got my leg out just in time and stepped off. That did not work. I tried it again and made sure this time he would not lie down. We only walked. I walked him for a few months in the round pen, around the property, up the road, and eventually on trails. He was easygoing and enjoyed being out and about. I had never separated him from his mom, and he knew we would always come back. Despite what many say, I think it unnecessary to separate foals from healthy moms, who are able to sustain milk production. Mother and foal naturally benefit emotionally from being together. When I look at my mare and her son and what an incredible bond they have to this day, it makes me wonder why someone would want to destroy this relationship. People have told me that the mother and colt will not recognize each other after a few months. However, I have seen horses recognize each other after a long separation, even to the point of nursing again if the mother still has milk. In the wild, a mare will naturally discontinue nursing when the next foal is born. Arbitrarily removing a foal at the tender age of six months has become a human prerogative, not based on anything natural or sensible.

My husband and I were doing less and less together. My life now belonged to the horses, and his belonged to his book. I tried to help him with the book, which resulted in arguments. The material was very complicated. I had trouble getting my mind around it, even after several readings. It was frustrating that he perceived this as a lack of willingness on my part. I was unable to meet his expectations. One day I will try again. I got a horse for Shambu, hoping he would ride. I ended up regretting it. My husband very much loved this horse but was not really interested in riding or taking care of him that much. While riding came naturally to me, I was not prepared to assist a beginning rider or to anticipate everything I would need to explain. Both of us blamed me for several incidents that discouraged Shambu. I have learned much from the regrets of that situation. I have since developed confidence with beginner riders, their learning needs, and what explanations are necessary prior to ground work and mounted work with a horse. I can teach them how to establish boundaries, how to move around a horse, how their body language speaks to a horse.

I spent more time alone and with my horses. Horses consumed my entire day, either at the ranch or at home. My mom had asked Shambu when I first got Shebrah, "Why did you let her get a horse?!" He told her, "I did not know I had a choice." My mom knew too well that I would have nothing else on my mind. I do not know if Shambu regretted having helped me with the path of the horse. It certainly caused us to grow apart. My husband's treatments, love, and patience had helped me with my physical and emotional health. He loved taking care of me and making me strong. Now the horses had taught me about leadership, and I became stronger. Through nobody's fault, I was no longer fulfilled in the relationship with Shambu.

I remember standing in the doorway of our yurt, making the decision I would do my own thing. We had never gone on vacation together, he had never come with me to visit my family in Germany, he was interested only in his book, spending all day in front of the computer. We did no longer attend prayer meetings together. The things that we had cherished together had fallen away; we had not nurtured them. Shambu was a man with a very, very big heart, always willing to help someone in need. He had the mind of a wizard and was a walking encyclopedia, able to answer in depth any question on any topic. Shambu was a healer with integrity, wisdom, and experience. He was older than I, our lives were at different stages, and our interests differed. I love and adore him, I respect and I honor him for everything he was and he stood for. He enjoyed solitude at home with the animals. I love this man. In retrospect, I would have done many things differently, but at the time I felt lonely and alone.

MY TRAVELS TO THE MAINLAND

In the summer of 2009, I started training to become a barefoot trimmer. I had five horses at the time, two of whom would go lame about three weeks after being shod and a third with a very flat coffin bone requiring regular barefoot trimming for an early break over. My barefoot Islandic/QH mare had excellent feet that would hold up to the rough lava terrain on Maui. In October of that year, one of my horses lost his front shoe. He could not take an imbalance for more then a day without becoming lame. My farrier was unable to come out, so I decided to pull the shoes myself. I pulled everyone's shoes. I decided to enroll in a training program requiring both study and practicum with different mentors. Because our group only had one mentor on Maui, I traveled to California. I had to go to the German Embassy to extend my passport, and the only embassy for the Pacific was in San Francisco. I visited a former German classmate there while renewing my passport. Then I drove to Chico to mentor with a woman in northern California. I took her anatomy course and enjoyed participation in trims for her private clients and horses at rescue centers. I stayed in Oroville, where I reconnected with my friend, Laurel, also from Maui. We spent some evenings together, going out for Chinese food and sharing stories and experiences.

Next I went to Nevada, where I stayed with another mentor and learned from her. I had been there only one day when it began to snow. We trimmed in the freezing cold. She fitted me with hand and foot warmers and made sure I was not freezing. We took turns trimming, because whoever held the horse and did not trim got cold quickly. It was the first big winter storm, and it stranded many people in airports and on highways. We worked on mules, mustangs, and her clients' horses. I particularly remember one mustang, because every time I changed position, he thought I was a new person. He would not allow me to touch him, and I had to start all over again. Little Amy, the mule living with him, took advantage of the situation and dragged my shawl and hat through the dirt after I removed them. She had way too much fun, because she knew I could not go after her! Leslie and I had a fabulous time and made ourselves comfortable at home at night. It was so nice to be able to stay with her! She also showed me how to take hay samples to test sugar, protein and mineral content.

Next, I drove to a valley north of Reno to study with Cindy, a vet who belonged to our barefoot trimming group. My GPS took me so far out of the way that I was fortunate not to get lost in the deep snow! It was a beautiful journey, though. Upon reaching her house, I was greeted by some huskies who were just fine with the cold and snow and some wolves that were fenced into their own area. Then there were her horses. I stayed at Cindy's home. We pulled shoes on a laminitic horse and trimmed various horses, including some mustangs. One night the temperature became too low to continue trimming. Instead, we stayed indoors and worked on reading radiographs correctly. I read many different radiographs, becoming skilled at finding foot pathologies. The forecast was for continued cold and more snow. I was scheduled with a clinic in California to learn about barefoot boots. I called the other mentor with whom I wanted to travel. She said that the pass was closed and I should come to her place. She would teach me instead. She said her husband was coming home for the weekend, and because he was gone for weeks at a time she wanted to spend time with him. Could I come Monday? It was no problem for me. I was grateful for her willingness to teach, so I could advance in my training.

I checked into a hotel. While using the computer, I overheard the conversation of four women at a table behind me. They were discussing horses and a clinic they were attending for the week. The concierge introduced me to the group, so we could share our experiences. So I ended up talking with Kim, Barbara, Wyoma and Jane about the course they were taking. It was about the therapeutic use of horses. Kim had her own ranch in Washington and did therapeutic riding with kids who had emotional and physical problems. On her laptop, she showed me a video of her granddaughter with horses. I was impressed. The little girl was only three years old and was quite firm with her four legged friends. Barbara had retired from the Navy and was now teaching leadership to corporations and women wanting to use the horse as a tool for teaching leadership. Again, I was impressed. Wyoma had her own cattle ranch in Montana, where she did therapy with at-risk Youth. They would send the most impossible toughest kids to her, and she was gifted enough to rehabilitate most of them. And there was Jane, who was a family therapist learning to use horses to augment her therapeutic techniques.

I was fascinated. I had always wanted to do therapeutic riding with children. I had had a dream about it years ago. We talked late into the night, and I expressed interest in what each of them was doing and in the program. We planned to go to dinner the next night. In the morning I met Barbara at breakfast. She was sitting at a table by herself and invited me over since I was also alone. We shared some thoughts, and I told her about myself. She had to leave for the clinic, and I spent the day shopping and enjoying the spa at the hotel. That night, I met the entire group after the weather had caused the clinic to end early. It was their last night. I met some people with whom I shared acquaintances on Maui. We had fun exchanging memories about places and people we had in common. I spent more time with the four women I had met, and each invited me to her home, should the opportunity ever present itself. I had to head out early the next morning to make it to Leslie's place, where I would learn about barefoot boots.

So I made my way back to Leslie's home, travelling on icy roads and heavy snow. I arrived after dark, ready to rest. I learned about the different kinds of boots, how to put them on, and how to disassemble each model for repair. I learned which boots to use for different conditions, rehabilitation, hoof shapes, and terrains. I took boots apart and put them back together; I learned how to order them, what to order, and which spare parts to have in stock. I stayed a little longer, changed my departure flight to Reno instead of California and headed back to Maui.

As much as I loved the time I spent in the high desert of Nevada, I did not fit in with most of the people. Perhaps a longer visit would have changed this impression. However, I was pleased with the connections I had made and did plan on visiting Kim and Barbara by the next summer.

MY DREAM "WHERE THE DESERT MEETS THE CEDAR"

∾

I returned to Maui and started trimming my own horses and those at the ranch. I picked up some other clients. Trimming different horses was good experience. My own horses were easy because I knew them well. The ranch horses were fairly easy for the same reasons. I worked on a few challenging hoof pathologies. I loved the horses I had worked with for the last 2 and half years and gave them my best. I was able to maintain an optimal trimming cycle, which is crucial to the outcome. Initially, I worked with some difficult situations. I worked with founder, laminitis, horses not trained to stand still, and horses whose hoof care had been neglected. The variety instilled increasing confidence.

One morning I awoke from a dream. I had searched for where I wanted to be. The barefoot journey had been merely a means to learn, grow, meet like-minded people, and connect with those who could point me in a direction. I enjoyed the horses, but now became centered on the right location. Where did I want to be? Where did I want to live my life? What do I want my life to look like? I awoke from the dream hearing very clearly, "You need to be where the desert meets the cedar." It sounded mysterious. It sounded true. It felt true. Where in the world would that be? I went on the Internet and researched desert and cedar and asked people, "Where does the desert meet the cedar," only to receive questioning looks. I tried to explain my dream and soon gave up. I realized it was mine to figure out. I trusted that I would find signs along the way directing me where to turn, and where to go. I realized I would not find it during an Internet search. I asked clairvoyants and counselors, looked at astrology and numerology, and came up with no answer.

Then in the spring, I called Kim and Barbara to ask if I could visit now rather than in the summer. I had to get off the Island for a bit to relieve stress and look for clarity. I wanted to learn about the therapeutic riding at Kim's ranch and receive some advice from Barbara. I booked my flight, and Barbara picked me up in Portland, Oregon. I met her two adopted children, who were precious. Her boy went to Kim's Ranch to go riding. They lived near each other. I stayed at Barbara's place and spent the day at Kim's Ranch. Barbara and her husband loaned me their red Jeep, so I was independent. How nice of them and how lucky for me!

I was in awe of Kim's ranch. Her horses were grazing in a big pasture. It looked surreal. She said, "Go pick one and hop on its back." I pointed on a horse in the distance. She was a white mare with a special look about her. Kim said, "Misty, huh? Well, walk up to her; she will take care of you." So I walked to the horse who was grazing in the distance and who was now looking up at me. Kim had followed me from a slight distance. I said hello to Misty and let her sniff my hand and face. I stroked her neck gently and stood next to her, talking to her, telling her how beautiful she was and how wise she appeared. Kim asked me, "Well, are you getting on her?" She gave me a lift up, and I just sat there on Misty's back, thinking, "Am I crazy? I don't even know this horse." But I felt safe on Misty's bare back. She just stood there, and I put my arms around her neck. Then I sat up straight and squeezed my legs just a little bit, gently, and Misty walked on just as gently. It was a bit muddy in one area from the rain, and Misty picked her way carefully to firm ground. She just grazed along taking a few steps here and there. It was perfect. Kim walked away with the children and left us to ourselves. I told Misty about my situation at home and the problems I faced, and she seemed to listen. I cried and felt better. After a while I got off her back and walked back to the barn.

Kim did not have much going on, and I was able to ask her questions. I said, "Why did I choose Misty?" She looked at me with amused and questioning eyes. "Well, can't you figure it out yourself," is what that look meant. I felt like I had known Kim forever. I repeated the question. So Kim told me, "Well, Misty is really sweet and really gentle, she has done a lot of work in her life and she is a bit tired. She is an older very wise mare. But she can be feisty and have her own ideas. She is not a push over." I asked her, "Why did I choose her?" Her reply was fast: "Because you feel the same way." I was happy with this answer and at the same time I was not. I had to think about this. Kim told me I could do whatever I wanted, hang out with the horses, watch her children's program, or feel free to trim horses. I opted to trim, because I wanted to get all fifteen big horses and 8 miniature horses trimmed during the two weeks of my visit. I asked Kim who was in the most need of trimming.

Nothing in Kim's world is normal, and I mean that in a good way! So her reply to me was: "Well let's see who wants to be trimmed." I was not going to argue with her but I wanted to make sure I got the horses who most needed trimming. The horse that needed it the most came up; it was perfect. I had to laugh because it was so perfect. Ghost was his name. He was a beautiful Palomino with blue eyes. He had some issues with his back and Kim offered to hold him for me. So I got to work. I talked with him, telling him exactly what I was going to do. I trimmed all four feet while he dozed with his head on Kim's arm. I had take care with his back feet, but we got through it. I gave him many rests; he gave me very little trouble. Another horse, Jackson, had walked in with Ghost. Kim held Jackson while I trimmed him. His feet had become long, and he had some deformity from an old leg fracture. We accomplished the trim with no problem. I talked to him the whole time and remained calm with him. I had just put my tools away when I saw that Kim was crying. I asked her what was wrong. She said, "You don't know this, because I did not want to scare you, but no one has ever been able to trim those two horses. I can do it but, I am having a hard time. You just walk in and they doze off, giving you their feet with no problem, trusting you completely! If you don't know what to do with your life, girl, I don't know!!!" I was perplexed. I did not know what to say. I thanked her for the compliment. "I mean it! You have a gift!!! Use it!" she replied. We finished trimming for the day. We both were overwhelmed with emotion. We did some other things with the kids that day.

Over the next days we had fun going for trail rides through the forest, along the river, and across creeks. I watched Kim work with the children and the horses. She had an amazing way with both. When there were disputes between the kids she never interfered. Instead, she facilitated their own understanding of the real issues. She established clear boundaries coached with love and understanding. Kim did a thousand things at once. Although overwhelmed at times, she loved and excelled at her work. She answered all of my questions with full focus. We had long talks while sitting in the pasture, under equine surveillance. I had shared with Kim the situation with my husband. Kim shared some advice and asked questions to elicit my beliefs regarding integrity, honesty, values, and goals. She understood my situation, because she had worked with many children and adult survivors of emotional or physical abuse. Boundaries become porous if not established during early development. This predisposes a person to emotional triggers regarding manipulation, aggression, or anger. Such a person often repeatedly seeks similar situations for the comfort of familiarity. I started to see myself in this light. I had received frequent counseling throughout life in an effort to learn what might have happened to me. I could not remember much of my childhood, except having been lovingly raised by my parents and grandparents. My dad was very strict in terms of my education, and I dreaded coming home with perceivably bad grades. Could that have been it? I no longer cared and wanted to move beyond it, to be free again, to spread my wings and fly!

When I returned to Barbara's place each night I gave her foot rubs, and we would talk until late. She also helped me to see my strengths and talents, considering the many areas I had studied and goals I had accomplished. Some people had said, "You don't stick with anything". Perhaps that is what they have noticed, but my perspective differs. I live fully, find new experiences, explore, and enjoy adventures as a trail-blazer and pioneer. The occasional insecurity and doubt I experience help me grow by facing my fears and shortcomings. Although I flourish with some amount of routine, a life devoid of new challenges becomes a boring routine. Barbara drew a big circle on a big piece of paper, and I filled in all the things I had studied and done in my life. She said, "To me you are an Equine Specialist. But you are more than that." This clarified my gifts and talents.

At Kim's ranch I continued to trim horses, to observe her equine therapy with children, and to interact with her herd of horses. I honed skills for setting boundaries with intention. There are many ways to achieve a goal! We had barbeques and dinners at Kim's and Barbara's place.

I made connections and visited other ranches to inquire as to potential boarding, should I move my horses to this area. However, I saw no desert or cedar.

Toward the end of my stay, Barbara went to the high desert in Bend, Oregon for a Seminar at Crystal Peaks Youth Ranch. She invited me to come for the beautiful drive. It rained so hard during the whole drive that I could not see the beauty around me. Barbara pointed to distant sights that would have been visible on a clear day! But we had fun. I went with her to check out the place and stayed for the introduction. The couple who had started the Rehabilitation Center years ago shared stories about how the horses and children heal each other, which brought tears to most in the room. Their accomplishment and team spirit were reflected in the joy we all felt. They had converted a cinder pit into a beautiful, flourishing, loving environment. The next class was titled, "How in the world am I going to do this," the "this" being starting a ranch to facilitate Therapeutic Riding. I wondered how I had ended up here. They were introducing their ideas on organizational success, recruitment and retention of volunteers, and selection of recipients for therapeutic services. But the most meaningful message I carried away was how they set their trust in God for guidance and help. I found myself staying for lunch and dinner, returning the next day, again staying for lunch before leaving to catch my return flight to Maui. I was inspired and very aware of how the Universe guides us and provides the path. Many coincidences really are not coincidences.

A DIFFERENT PATH
LAYS AHEAD

∽◦◦

I returned Maui with a new sense of having a goal. At the seminar, I had connected with people from Maui. I continued to trim horses and work for the ranch, all the while being happy that my time on Maui was coming to an end. All I needed was to find that place where the desert meets the cedar. Before I had left for Oregon, I had told my landlord of my wish to move to the mainland and of difficulties in the relationship with my husband. The landlord had offered me the cottage on our land for as long as needed. He reminded me not to rush a decision, offered any help I needed, and said he would miss me if I left. We had cared for his property for seven years. So now I moved into the cottage and acclimated to living alone. As good as I felt about relocating my belongings to my own space, both Shambu and I needed time to assimilate the change. What helped was that we cared enough for each other that we maintained our friendship.

Another turn of events changed my life. The ranch

did a complete staff turnover, laying off most of their employees, including me. After the initial shock, I realized that it was just the Universe telling me what my heart already knew. It was time to move on from a job with which I had become dissatisfied. It was time to find my new home. Meanwhile, my own trimming business sustained me.

FINALLY! THE DESERT
MEETS THE CEDAR

Once again I booked a ticket to the mainland. This time my destination was Colorado, where I had contacts. Friends thought I would love Colorado. In northern Colorado, I stayed with my long-time friend, Steve. We went to the Shambalah Buddhist Retreat Center in the mountains. It was peaceful, and I felt so good being in the mountains. On our return home, I suggested a short visit to New Mexico. We rented a car and had a lovely, rainy drive southward. As we approached New Mexico my heart began to sing!!! I could not contain my inexplicable joy. At Crestone, we turned off for an unplanned visit to an old friend, whom I had no idea how to find. Some hitchhikers who joined us turned out to also be close friends of this person. They showed us the way. John was there! Although on his way to look at a car he wanted to buy, he made time to welcome us and visit for a little while. He was a Hopi Elder and had taught the Hopi Prophecy that had been passed on to him. He had just returned from a conference and had put a beautiful story, Jack Hopper, on DVD. I bought the DVD, and we listened to it as we made our way to New Mexico, the Land of Enchantment.

We spent the night in Santa Fe, close to where a member of our barefoot trimming group lived. She invited me to visit, so we drove to her home the next morning. I wanted to make contacts and learn about the business in New Mexico. On arrival at her place, I was speechless. I had not felt so much at home in a long time, probably not since my arrival on Maui. I felt that I had been here before and had returned to see old friends. I so loved the red canyons and the smell of cedar and sage. There it was clearly: Where the desert meets the cedar. The trees were junipers, part of the cedar family with the same aroma. The people used it in ceremonies. I had prayed to find my home this time. Priscilla invited us in, and we spoke for a little while. She invited us to stay for as long as we wanted to. My friend and I discussed what to do next. I told him what he already knew, that I wanted to remain here rather than return to Colorado. We discussed logistics. He would drive the rental car back to Colorado, having assisted me in finding my home. He did not want to leave his cats alone for much longer. In the morning, Priscilla would drive me to the airport to rent another car, so I could be mobile.

I basked in morning awakenings to red canyons and nocturnal coyote song. The air smelled fresh and was pristine and clear. Priscilla was about to travel, so she gave me a key to her house, saying I could stay as long as I liked.

I planned to meet her in Los Angeles for a conference the following week. Meanwhile, I explored, longing to return each time I drove out of the area. I spent a night in Santa Fe, explored south of Albuquerque, drove through the Valles Caldera Preserve, and visited Chimayo, only to return to the Jemez area. I called Priscilla to inquire whether she knew anyone who might have room for my horses, my dog, and me. She said she knew someone who might have contacts. I called Ron, drove to his place and we talked. He said he had a guest cottage, and there was enough room in his barn for his four horses and mine. At the time I planned on bringing two horses. We instantly liked each other and felt this could work.

I returned to the house and thought about it. I went to the store, where I had a chance meeting with a woman to whom my old boyfriend had introduced me when I took his daughter riding at the resort. We had exchanged email. The woman offered me work, should I be serious about moving to New Mexico. At this time, I used my friend's tools, and trimmed some horses for this woman.

On my way home, I stopped at the store, where an older Indian man asked for a ride home to Jemez. With a recent knee replacement, he was unable to walk. He was grateful that I spoke with him and brought him home, as white people seldom took the time. He invited me into his simple home. When I told him of my wish to move to New Mexico, we had a prayer together. He asked how I knew, and I told him about my heart singing and hearing the birds singing a certain way. As we shared more, I realized I had been here before and had just returned.

The man showed me the reservation, where they grew which plants, and how they watered crops. He told me to be aware of certain signs and who my guides would be. I felt very blessed!

I enjoyed some time by the river and hot springs before catching my flight to Los Angeles. It was a big transition from a Paradise to three days at an airport hotel and a conference. I finally met a lot of the people in our barefoot trimming group. I learned about how the living condition of the Brumbee horses in Australia affected foot condition. Rather than spend a fourth night in the hotel, I called my friend Linda in San Diego to let her know I was driving south to visit her.

I enjoyed the drive along the coast, despite the traffic and development. Even the beautiful and tasteful ranch land of Rancho Santa Fe, could not compare to the raw and powerful open high desert of New Mexico. I knew in my heart that I did not belong in southern California. Linda kindly cooked for me and listened to me while I rested and recovered from the conference and all the travelling. The next morning, I met her two dogs and three horses, swam in her pool, and enjoyed the fragrance of her flower and herb gardens. We went for lunches and dinners. I met some of her very interesting friends, connected with some people in the race horse industry or who rescued race horses after they were done with the track. We even went to the races one day. Linda dressed me up with a dress, big hat, high heels, and an elegant purse, and off we went to the races. We had champagne and watched the horses betting. We were able to go behind the scenes, where the horses where kept before racing. I was shocked at the tied tongues and instruments that made the horses be still and be manageable before racing.

I made more contacts. It would be easier to start a business here than in the less wealthy area of northern New Mexico. We spent some days at Linda's home, during which time, while Carolyn's student interacted with the horses, Alethia captured the sessions on film. Carolyn's approach and results impressed me; in particular, I noted the enthusiasm with which these powerful creatures interacted with the humans. I asked this extraordinary woman what it would take for me to study with her. She said "You can just study with me, I like you." I offered to trim her horses. We became better acquainted over the next few days. I had extended my stay in order to find a place for my horses. This area offered a milder winter and the opportunity to learn from Carolyn. I was excited about assisting with her approaching clinics. I put my resume together for Linda's friend to post on a horse list. I drove around the area, searching for a living situation for myself, my horses, and my dog. I visited the one woman who responded to my posting and immediately liked her and her place. She had two horses and two dogs. She had recently purchased the property for herself, her two horses, and two dogs and was on the verge of clearing dead avocado trees and fencing a pasture. She had a hay barn and a room to rent. I could live near Carolyn and Linda rather than feeling completely alone in a new area. I could live near my horses. Deborah and I had a lot in common, she was kind and loving, and we both thought this was a workable living situation. I left my few travel items at Deborah's home, planning to return in about six weeks with my remaining belongings from Maui. I was relieved that my horses could rest when they deplaned, rather than enduring an additional several travel days. I could study with an incredible horse woman without fear and struggle for survival. After a few days at Linda's home, I returned to Maui, pleased at having accomplished my mission. I knew my next destination. Although sad about not returning to New Mexico, I thought I had found the perfect landing spot.

A CYCLE COMES TO COMPLETION

~⊙~

I returned to Maui to pack and organize for my journey. The twelve years during which I had lived on Maui seemed like the perfect cycle. The decision to depart left me heartbroken while yet anticipating the new beginning. I had deeply loved Maui and its people for twelve years.

I started to give away those who would not accompany me to my new life. Parting with the first horse was so difficult, I was not sure I could go through with it. But he found a beautiful home whose owner he had known since he was foaled. He would be loved and cared for until the end of his days. He would be pampered, ridden, and lavished with more attention than I was ever able to give him. An old injury would heal over a longer time than the six weeks I had given myself to prepare to leave. One morning I trailered Billy and all of his belongings to his new ranch. I was thankful to the friend who took him in and yet very sad. I would visit Billy a few more times, though I had no doubt as to his wellbeing.

The next concern was to find a home for my eleven-year-old gelding, Sammy. He had foundered from an old injury. The beautiful, big-hearted horse found a nine-year-old girl who felt blessed to call Sammy her own. He became a pasture mate for her older white pony, Willow. I left her with Sammy's belongings and his trimming instructions. I could only pray to Creator to take care of the ones I left behind.

I sold my trailer and some of the belongings I could not take with me, but mostly gave everything away. I packed my life, including the tack and saddles for the rest of my horses, whom I would ship in a 4-by-4-by-4-foot pallet. It was freeing to reduce my life to this small amount. The more I gave away the freer I felt.

For weeks, I cried every night. When I thought there could be no more, the tears never stopped. It is unusual for me to cry so much and so out of control, but I gave up trying to stop it. My heart physically hurt, and I felt soreness throughout my upper body. My tears were for all previous relationships and the emotions left unresolved from my marriage in Germany. My tears were about sacrificing my marriage to Shambu, a relationship I had really wanted. Shambu and I had experienced relationship trouble for the past three years. Now I had consciously chosen to be alone rather than continue to run to new relationships.

I was also leaving this land and the friends. Gazing over the ocean from my cottage, I saw the West Maui Mountains and the most beautiful orange, pink, and red sunsets. Despite the worst draught since 1937 causing livestock to suffer and my horses to forage afar, I loved this beautiful land on Kealakapu , "The Sacred Path." In the seven years that Shambu and I had lived here with our animals, I had seen owls and deer daily. I knew every rock, every tree, and every sound. I could walk this land in the dark without fear, despite tales of Nightmarchers, spirits who had not made the transition from their bodies to the next world. We had built our dream on this land, living in a yurt surrounded by a native forest. I knew everyone living on our road after seven years of sharing our stories, hopes, and concerns. I had enjoyed riding my horses up the road on Friday afternoons for fresh organic vegetables and share life stories.

However, I had also craved more open space and endless riding trails. For years, I had talked of moving to the mainland. This was a life changing moment. I had decided to leave my Maui life behind. Despite my fear, I knew I could do it, as I had when leaving Germany. The difference this time was that I was taking three horses and my dog, Kalima, to go alone into the unknown.

The horses would need transfer from the barge to boarding in Oahu and then be boarded onto the flight to Los Angeles. Kalima and I had a flight the same day, so I could meet the horses in Los Angeles and haul them to San Diego. Health certificates and vaccinations were valid only within a narrow timeframe. I had to arrange for a rental vehicle and a dog kennel. Finally, it was September 12, 2010. I was nervous. I tried to remain calm and present with my animals, to instill confidence for their journey. We had talked about the trip and what to expect at each transition. They knew I would meet them after crossing the ocean. I had committed to honor the request of my six-year-old gelding, who did not want to be handled by men. I promised to be there to drive with the company picking up the horses in Los Angeles. I knew my 22-year-old mare, Shebrah, would take care of her 6-year-old son, Kyros, and my little 5-year-old half Islandic/half QH, Glory. They had to be unsupervised on the barge for 16 hours. I was grateful that the cowboys had insisted that I acclimate my horses to being tied for hours, so I would find them where I left them. It helped mitigate the fears from stories of broken necks and long bones from horses jumping out of box stalls. Workers at the dock assured me that conditions were calm, and that wind and waves should be no cause for concern. Friends helped clean the box stall and put in fresh shavings. We rearranged the stall dividers so that Glory could not bite Kyros. There were buckets of water and nets filled with hay. I could only pray for their safety. The fork lift came and picked them up. They munched hay while being driven a foot or so off the ground to the barge headed for Oahu. There they stood in their box stall between stacked containers and cars. I did not want to let go. One more time, one last time, I wanted to check on them. I was allowed to go to them. The dock worker understood that my babies were embarking on a journey! I appreciated his attempts to instill confidence before he had to clear the dock.

With no time to return home, I drove the short distance to Paia, a little beach town. There, I showered at a friend's house, changed, and went for a very last walk on the beach at Paia Bay. I met another very dear friend who wanted to fare me well. Then, I had to go. My husband took us to the airport, made sure Kalima and I got checked in, and took care of my truck. It had to be shipped later, being two inches too tall for the next shipment. I never thought this would be my last time to see Shambu!

I never, expected Kalima, my calm dog, to be so frightened or to shake so much. I wished I had tranquilizers for him, but it was too late now. I stayed with him until I could no longer remain in his area. I boarded and the woman handed me a red ticket that told me Kalima was aboard the same flight. I had done all I could do. I had only to wait and pray for the safety of my animals. We arrived in LAX early the next morning. It seemed that I waited forever for Kalima' kennel. The worker would not allow me to use the luggage cart. The rental car company did not open until 8:00 a.m. How could this be? I had reserved the car for 5 a.m. Why would they not tell me they weren't open at this time? Using the Internet on my phone, I booked another rental car with a different company. I took the kennel apart to fit it into the SUV, and Kalima and I drove to San Diego. I was exhausted. We stopped at a restaurant for breakfast and shared a Spinach Omelette with baked potatoes, drank plenty of water and coffee to wake up, and drove the rest of the way. Finally. Our new home.

Deborah, my landlady and roommate, welcomed us. We crashed and slept. Kalima slept for days in the dark closet. His two little new-found friends, Bronte and Jake, hardly saw him in the beginning.

Now it was a matter of waiting for the horses. I left for LAX at 9 p.m. two days later to pick up the horses at one in the morning. I returned my rental car and waited. 250 cows had been shipped from the Big Island on the same plane because of the bad drought. It was sad to see these skinny animals. Then two pallets with horses arrived. One pallet was mine! Here they were. They looked good. Shebrah concerned me a little bit. She was hungry and thirsty and appeared dehydrated and stressed. The younger horses looked better. I loaded them onto the trailer, where I fed and watered them. The people were friendly, but I was glad to be there in person to care for the horses after such a long trip! On the freeway, the driver elected not follow my GPS. I think we got to San Diego via Palm Springs, taking over five hours on windy roads instead of 2 and a half. There was nothing I could do. I just felt so sorry for my animals.

We finally arrived at our destination. I put them in the arena, watered them, and fed them. Kyros and Glory laid down to rest, and good old Mama Shebrah, who was most exhausted stood guard over them. She so needed rest. I stayed with them, but she would not lie down. Eventually everyone settled in. I was so glad I had decided to take Shebrah with me. I loved that mare. She had been my first horse. Although she was older, and I had considered leaving her on Maui, I could not part with her. Every time I contemplated leaving her I cried, so I took her. She has taught me so much!

After I had rested, I sat down with my landlady to read my email and let people know I was okay. Deborah told me I should rest for a few days before doing anything. Twenty minutes later, she drove me to buy the car I had found on the Internet. I had to take the California driving test, register the car, unpack, get settled, rest, care for my animals, and think about work. The rest of my belongings arrived after a couple of weeks, and I was able to work a little here and there. My mom flew in from Germany to reassure herself of my wellbeing after this big transition. She helped me, and we had fun exploring the area even though it was still unfamiliar to me. She helped me pick up my truck once it arrived.

In record high temperatures, with the switch from pasture grass to hay, with an unaccustomed water source, Shebrah colicked one night. As her condition deteriorated, I tried without success to find an available vet. My mare rolled and rolled, I walked, only to have her collapse and roll again. She became cast in the arena panels, and I could not free her. I sent my mom up to the road for help. Some young people and their mom finally helped us to get Shebrah unstuck. Still no vet. Some new friends whom I had helped with their horse called every vet in the area, and finally a helpful female vet showed up. She gave pain medication, mineral oil, and Chinese herbs. Kalima was there with us, licking Shebrah's eyes while she was down. My animals were always close, but through this journey they became inseparable, caring for each other beyond what I had ever seen.

In the following weeks, we all struggled with record heat. I started to study with Carolyn Resnick, whom I had met during the summer I stayed with Linda. She and

Alethia had worked on pictures for Carolyn's book while Carolyn's Columbian student worked with Linda's horses. We had shared daily activities and grown close. Carolyn's gift is the magical and effortless manner displayed during her work with horses. It appears easy until we students try it.

Despite my growing success during this time, I would see the red canyons of New Mexico every time I closed my eyes. When I told old friends about it, I realized I had left my heart in New Mexico. The Southern California climate was ideal for our transition from the tropics, and the plentiful work available eased my concern for survival. My horses also had good living conditions on the same property where I lived. I had finally registered my cars after dealing with the requirements of the state. I was prepared for a mild winter, and it made no sense to move. Yet, I could not erase the longing in my heart. It was as if a magnet pulled me eastward. I weighed my options.

One morning I awoke knowing beyond doubt that I would move to New Mexico. The clarity brought joy to my heart. I called my New Mexico acquaintances, including Ron. He said the little Adobe cottage had just become vacant, my horses could stay in the barn, and my dog was welcome whenever we were ready. I also called the woman who had offered some work doing trail rides. During the slow winter season, I could supplement trail ride work by offering massage at the resort. I called the vet to arrange for the paperwork required for interstate horse transport. Trailering three horses from southern California to New Mexico was more than I wanted to undertake alone. I was uncomfortable accepting such a big favor from a recent acquaintance who offered. So I called an older friend from Maui, Lorenzo, who was currently visiting Los Angeles. He had been wondering how to spend his remaining week before flying back to Maui. He was eager to accompany me, but it meant my foregoing the much anticipated ten-day clinic with Carolyn. My animals and I were packed and ready to go within three days. Lorenzo arrived to help with the last of the packing.

We sat in the pasture, gazing at planets and stars, and Lorenzo, told me about the constellations. We shared stories, talked about the journey, debating the longer southern route with fewer weather surprises versus the northern route through Flagstaff. People had warned me against the northern route and the risk of being stuck in snow with three horses and a dog. Over dinner, we researched horse stables enroute. We had a prayer, gave thanks, and asked for a safe journey. We planned to leave at 4:00 a.m. to avoid traffic. In the early morning, I made coffee and tea and packed healthy snacks and drinks. My favorite student and good friend had given me delicious thing for the trip and had even thought about Kalima! We loaded the horses. Kalima was already in the truck, very excited and not willing to be left behind! In the dark, we headed north, where no snow was forecast.

On this new morning, with the sun just rising, we left without traffic problems. We stopped for short breaks along the way. Just after noon we crossed into Arizona and found a nice place off the Highway to break for lunch. We took the horses out of the trailer for food, water, and a walk through the sand dunes. It felt good to stretch our own legs. People camping close by chatted with us. It felt good. We celebrated having left California. I am not sure why it felt so good, but it did. I wanted real people around me, grounded, not superficial. I wanted to leave the hectic life of California with all its rules. As we left the area, I momentarily got the trailer stuck in a small dip in the sand. I did not think much of it at the time.

We continued on, arriving in Kingman by early afternoon. We put up the horses at a ranch just off the highway. They put shavings down for the horses and put us up in a cabin that supposedly sleeps four. The two of us with Kalima barely fit into that cottage, but we were fine. The heater kept us comfortable. After caring for the horses, we decided to have dinner at a recommended Mexican restaurant in town. That is when we discovered that the mishap with the sand dent had jammed the trailer hitch. We could not release the trailer without risking a difficult realignment in the morning. So we had to bring the trailer along. We had margaritas and a wonderful spicy dinner and lots of laughter and fun! What a journey. We were riding on fairy dust and being pulled by angels. Everything had come together in such a magical easy way. I felt so supported by the Universe. The ease with which thing came together on the journey told me I had made the right decision. Later, we took the horses from the round pen, put them into their corrals, and fed and watered them. Then we headed straight to bed in anticipation of an early start. We gave thanks.

I awoke early for a hot, steaming shower. Clean and

fresh, I packed, cleaned the trailer, and replaced shavings for the next leg of the journey. We loaded the horses and headed out into the cold and darkness. I loaded the horses up and my friend and I headed out. Lights shining into my eyes made driving difficult. It was hard to see the tracks left by larger trucks, and my truck and trailer did not travel in the same tracks. Lorenzo was more accustomed to driving, so travel was faster once he took over. I was glad though to have driven a good part of the journey. It gave me confidence that I could actually do it. I enjoyed the wide open spaces through the desert. We had no music, because the radio had shorted out the first time we tried to use it; so we sang. We pulled off the highway to feed the horses and then continued on our way. We had allocated three days for our trip but rolled in to the ranch at 2 p.m. on the second day. We had arrived! I was home. Oh, did my heart beat with excitement and joy! I could barely believe it. I gave thanks. We put the horses in the barn with their new friends. We fed and watered them, unloaded some things, and left the rest where it was. I crashed early on the couch, my friend awoke me so I could sleep in my new bed, and I slept until morning. I left him to make his own dinner from the few items we had brought. I was too exhausted to eat. Was I lucky Lorenzo was so easy going!

NEW BEGINNING

❦

I awoke at first light. Through my bedroom window, I saw the Junipers in my back yard and the mountains around me. Joy overwhelmed me. I had arrived. We checked on the horses, made friends with the new dogs on the property, had breakfast and just enjoyed the morning. While the horses rested, we could explore. Lorenzo had previously lived nearby, still had friends here, and always enjoyed the area. We spent some time at the hot springs he knew of close to my new home, soaking and enjoying the mountains and serenity. We had prayers of thanks and just enjoyed being there and being in each other's company. There is nothing like a friend with whom you can share either silence or conversation, sharing anything, and knowing you are heard. We took in the beautiful drive through the Valle Caldera, where I saw Lorenzo's old ranch. We shared beautiful moments, reflecting on life and loved ones who had passed. May they be blessed.

We had lunch at an old brick place with so much character, apparently unchanged over the last thirty years.

The same owner sat at the same table visiting with friends, drinking wine, and enjoying the good life. We had a very delicious Mexican lunch there before continuing on to Santa Fe to visit Lorenzo's friends. On our return to the cottage, we rearranged furniture, cleaned up, stored belongings, and felt increasingly at home. We watched stars from the swing on the front porch. I suddenly realized that I had lost my necklace with a beautiful pendant. The pendant had been a wedding gift from dear friend. She had received it from a Maori Chief in New Zealand. Not only did it have special meaning, but it was a uniquely shaped mother of pearl piece. The necklace that held the pendent had been a gift from my grandmother. It was white gold and came with a ring and another beautiful pendant. My grandmother had passed away a couple of years ago, and I liked wearing a necklace that reminded me of her. My heart sank. What a beginning, to lose something so precious at the sacred hot springs. I called Shambu to tell him what had happened. As usual, he remained calm and knew what to say. "Oh, that is great. You made a wonderful offering, and perhaps it has some relevance to your new beginning. Let go of the old." I was not happy. I could see his point, but I was very attached to the necklace. Shambu said, "Well how do you know it is no longer there? Did you look again? If it really belongs to you it will still be there. Check on it in the morning. "

I asked Lorenzo if he would look for my pendant in the morning. He was willing, as it would be great to visit the hot springs again. The next morning we took a different route. We chose a four wheel drive road that connected to the highway and had the most beautiful drive. We stopped along the way to take pictures. Finally we climbed to the hot springs. There was my necklace but not the pendant. I focused on the gray black rocks where we had found the necklace in the dirt. There it was, upside down. The shiny side was hidden, and it was scratched. Someone must have stepped on it and pushed it into the gravel. Nobody had noticed it. I picked it up. The top had broken from the tiny ring that held the piece to the necklace. I was so thankful. I felt so much better knowing nobody had taken it, and it was truly mine. The sacred hot springs had kept it for me and perhaps blessed it. We slipped into the hot springs, feeling wonderful about the pendant, our trip, and the world in general! We stayed a while before returning to "my" village, where the Native Americans were having a dance for the lady of Guadelupe. Lorenzo planned to meet friends who would take him to Santa Fe for some time together. We arrived at the Plaza, where the dancers in colorful costumes where dancing to drumming and songs, rhythmically tapping their feet to the drums making the jingles join the rhythm. There were Spanish dances and Native American traditional dances in bear costumes and eagle feathers. It was beautiful. As soon as we arrived, Lorenzo's friends wanted to leave having waited all morning while we were at the hot springs. The good bye after our time spent together felt abrupt and not quite right. He was gone. I felt sad.

I returned to the Plaza and watched dances all afternoon. I met Hinako, Ron's wife, and her friend. She took us to one of her student's homes where the women had made a feast of delicious dishes, cakes, sodas, and cookies. We sat down and joined them. There were grandmothers and daughters serving together. They were proud to tell us who was participating in the dances and who was dressed in which costumes. I returned to the Plaza to watch more dances, bought some turquoise earrings with a silver feather, and returned home. I missed Lorenzo after spending so much time together. We talked on the phone and decided that I would pick him up in Albuquerque the next day for a few more days of visiting before his return flight to Los Angeles. Then I took him to the airport, where we said proper A hui ho's – Until we meet again's, as the Hawaiians say.

SPREADING MY OWN WINGS

❧

Now my own journey began. Being unsure what to do with myself, I kept busy organizing things, changing addresses, setting up a bank account, getting my own post office box in the village, researching New Mexico's massage license requirements, and applying for a transcript of my massage license in Hawaii. It felt good to set up my life here where I wanted to be. I drove to the Motor Vehicle Division as they call it in New Mexico and again needed different documents than what California had required. I called Connie, the woman who had offered me work with the trail rides. She was in Arizona, because her husband passed away from a stroke the previous night. What a fate! She gave me her co-worker and employee contacts and thanked me for showing up at a perfect time. I felt so sad for Connie. I did not know her well enough to be really able to help her at this time, but I drove to her feed store, made contact with the people and co-workers, gave them my contacts and told them I was available whenever they needed me. I went to the resort to learn about the operation, the horses, and the trails. It was a most beautiful place. The trail rides went through the Indian reservation, either through sand dunes and high desert or along the Rio Grande River between Cottonwood Trees. What a serene place! The sacred rock that told the Indians where to settle was my orientation to find back to the Stables, no matter where I was. It was a great place to work. The people I worked with were patient and let me create my own experiences without micro managing. I thrive in such an environment, light hearted and easy going, all striving to help each other.

One day I had saddled and tied my trail horse, Silver, to the rail while doing other chores and saddling horses for the next ride. I tried to not tie horses tightly, because one of the horses had pulled back recently. I returned and saw a white horse lose and roaming toward the fields behind the Stables. I pointed at him and commented, "There is a horse loose". Ernesto replied, "It's your horse!" So I caught him as quickly as possibly, but returned with the reins Silver had broken during his escapade. Ernesto and Horacio made no big deal of it and were happy to fix the reins for me. "Just don't let it happen again!" I felt silly, but it was another good lesson in taking personal responsibility for my actions.

The car I had recently purchased in California had yet to make its way to New Mexico. I considered whether I should fly back to retrieve it or find someone to drive it to New Mexico. I did not want to repeat the long drive alone. I needed to get settled, figure out my work situation, and be available. My friend, Joe, who had offered to transport my horses and me to New Mexico, now offered to bring my car. This time I gladly accepted. He also brought the remaining belongings that I had been unable to sell in California. I wanted everything in one place. So he surprised me for New Year, and I started the 2011 with my car and belongings in New Mexico. I was not alone to start the New Year. We celebrated our friendship with margaritas of the special Tequila reserved for giving thanks for safe round-ups and cattle branding. Once again I was grateful for friends who had helped with my transitions, offering love and support. Many believed in me and gave me strength to move on. Some have told me, "Oh, I am not worried about you! You will do just fine," which gave me strength and confidence. In addition, some gave me actual physical support. I don't know how to thank everyone enough who has helped me in this journey!

I also know that there are those who are jealous and don't want me to succeed because of their own fears and failure to fulfill their own dreams and heart desires. I understand that it is a scary place to be, and that it takes a lot of courage to make the first step. I would like to give the people who seek the truth of their own heartfelt desires the wisdom I have acquired with time and experience. When you come from your heart and you follow your heart, the Universe will support you. You will receive the help you need. You must do your part, though, and be available for opportunities. You must exert the energy required to move forward. You must project intent in order to receive help. The path requires faith and a full commitment to your goal. The Universe will fill in the details once you commit to your decision. The result will be much more powerful, perhaps different, often more beautiful then you could have imagined!!!

FOLLOWING A
HIGHER CALLING

Having said this, I have embarked on a new journey into the unknown with trust and faith. Although unknown right now, it is amazing to know that I have just started a life mission that is supported by the Ascended Masters. I now realize that through each step I have taken, for which I have chosen to show up, say yes, and made decisions to say yes, and move forward, they have watched and found me worthy of helping on Earth and in other realms. I feel honored.

I had been comfortably alone for about a year and half, focusing on my work, my animals, and my self-realization. After so many clearings and so much work on myself, I was ready to come out of my self-inflicted isolation. My drive to work seemed longer and longer, and I decided to put my house on the market. I had recently come across a program and felt very drawn to it. Initially, I tried to ignore the calling, as I felt I could not afford it. However, I checked with my higher self and continued to receive a very strong YES. I charged the first part, an interview, to my credit card. The number of students was already clear. I went through the interview, which was really a Transcendental Rebirthing session. It cleared my field of things like military presence in my field, Shambu's expectation that I "had to write a book," and his needing to let me fall in love again. I felt quite clear after the session but did not know yet if I would be accepted into the program.

Three days later, I received an email from a man whom a client had wanted me to meet for many months. The timing of this email got my attention, as it seemed to be divine right order and divine right timing. It took three days for me to respond, because I kept checking with my higher self about whether this was my life partner and soul mate. I told the Universe that I was quite happy alone; I did not want to go through another heartbreak as I was just recovering from all this grief; I did not want to waste time on something that would not work. And yet I continued to receive a "Yes, this is your life partner and soul mate." I finally responded. How could I not trust my higher self?! We emailed, we met, and I knew that my higher self had been right. How do you tell somebody when you first meet? I gave it a little time but not much, and he took it very gracefully. What a joy in my heart! I felt that I had known him forever. I was comfortable and felt no need to hold anything back or think about what I could or could not say.

Then I asked my teacher if I had been accepted into the Ascended Master Teaching Academy. Indeed, I was accepted. As a matter of fact I felt I had been signed up instead of signing up myself. I was called, I realized. I had to trust this decision, once again asking my higher self and getting a yes. Once I get clear on something I move forward without hesitation. My very first session was incredible. There it was: my life mission revealed. What a journey ahead of me!! And the beautiful glow in my heart! What a gift to be able to be in contact with these amazing Ascended Masters!

Blessed Be Child of the One

My Name is Lord Kuthumi, and I have been looking forward to welcoming thee into the realms here we all access, to learn and support the universal manifestation of the one

I have been asked to tell you next steps to take as you begin this journey where we will guide thee to establish strongly thy life mission

where you will share my messages to the world

and will repattern the consciousness regarding animals

death and life

Thy life is to be a manifestation of the Masters on Earth

thou Must teach

and learn to listen the communication of the animal kingdom and speak the language of grief to others

assist others to transcend the passing of a loved one

an animal

a friend

through several techniques we will give

all is and has been performed by thee in thy different manifestations

thou are with us

and in many realms simultaneously working on this

now child of love, listen well the next 21 days are to be a major eradication of old beliefs, patterns and studies that no longer fit the academy

thy job is to journal and visualize a school

a physical school where people come and listen,

practice yoga

and heal from grief

as they get activated in

1. love for nature

2. inner ascension

3. reawakening of the empowered self

is this clear?

Claudia: yes

now thou must know I have been assigned as thy guardian over the academic year

every student, will have its own guardian

and ascended field mentor

if thou allow I will like to stay

Claudia: I feel very very honored. Thank you, Lord Kuthumi

I now close this orb of communications and ask thee to begin absolute mastery in thy practice of journaling feelings...around others, animals and thee alone

as through the journal we shall speak more

and the mastery of supporting others to manage and master the emotional realm

which is essential for grief

will take place

blessed be child of the one

Kuthumi

Teacher: Alright...

There is another Master coming

Right now what I desire to do is if you have questions you may ask them now... or if you chose we continue as we were doing

Claudia: I only have one question but we can continue to not disturb the flow. Where is the location of this school going to be? I just put my house on the market and would like to figure out where next.

Teacher: o.k

great question lets offer them to the space and see what the masters say

Claudia: great

Blessed Be Daughter

This Is Babaji

Well we meet again

And again

And again

and thy questions are to be answered

as thou will move out of thee place and state thou live

the school will be shown in time

the area will shift

as thou move in to an area of absolute animal lovers

and thou encounter thy life partner and move together

the reasons on how and why are not yet to be solved
neither a worry thou must ever have

the life that you are about to manifest is the one you
have always dreamed of and more

as thou are a member of the academy of consciousness

thou are a master in training

we all are

and as thou walk with this vision

of being a master

of being present

I desire to visualize that all beliefs

all

all

all of them

begin to fade

no name for the rose

no name for a she

or a we

labelessness is your first assignment

wherever you walk

to whomever you talk to

think this:

I see, feel, think beyond labels

I recognize your essence

I am.

Now, besides all what Kuthumi has asked, I want you to be initiated in kriya yoga

my fellow friends here in the different dimensions laugh as I like all our students to go through this process

yes we have sense of humor

we are masters

and we are students

you and I are from the same lineage

of heart resonance

and thus we feel at ease and an ancient recognition

thy path is to show others this

resonance

heart awakening

in thy mission steps

thou must create a portal

that announces the work you do

and write this down:

Living Beyond Grief

Liberating thyself from the cords of the past

Meeting the face of present joy here and now

Teacher: Claudia, there is a pause in the space.. In my experience when this happens the masters want you to ask

Claudia: Have I met my life partner?

yes

:)

Claudia: Lady Nada pointed out a 3300 acres ranch above Santa Barbara by the beach—and asked me to go there and walk the Ranch. Is this a possible place for the school?

Now the moment of revelation is at hand

yes California is where thou must be

and where the animal lovers will come

I desire thee to go up in the mountains

and visit Ramakrishna

a friend of mine

in meditation thou will receive further instructions

the Vedanta temple

go and meet him there

he will be waiting for thee

in silence receive a transmission

your life mission has begun

and has been blessed and accepted as one that can change the world frequencies within the ascended masters realms

not all missions are accepted as this

some are good for the 3d

some for a certain human purpose

yours has the capacity to create impact contribution
in all realms

thus

we have summoned thee

we need help

and we give thee ours

all will unfold

and in days of doubt

we will be there to remind thee

that

thou

shall

never

ever again

be alone

blessed be daughter

Babaji

I was rendered speechless. It rang so true and so right. I had seen this school they were talking about in a vision when I started massage school on Maui. I had started to bring a whole group of people, a team, together to make it happen. It was right in front of me. But the land on which I based this project was sold, and I had literally no foundation. I was confused and unable to understand how something this clear and almost tangible could not happen in the 3d. It was a heartbreak, and since this dream had fallen apart I had become unwilling to talk about things close to my heart. Now they told me – it will manifest!

Lady Nada had already given me nine steps for my grief-processing program. Apparently the Ascended Masters were in unison about this! Now I needed to get started with the assignments given by Lord Kuthumi, Babaji and Lady Nada!

INTO THE UNKNOWN

As I am sitting here, getting ready to send this manuscript to the publisher, I am realizing that everything is in the flow in exact right timing and divine order. The above messages, which I received about one year ago, are coming true. I have graduated from the Ascended Masters Teaching Academy and have created the Radiant Soul Sanctuary online for people to heal from grief, find joy in their lives and empower themselves. This Sanctuary will take physical form as well once we are in California. I am so looking forward to this that my heart begins to jump! I hope to welcome you there!

I have met my soul mate and life partner, Tony, an amazing loving soul who completely and without question supports me in this life mission, and has given me trust and courage by his calm presence and the things he shoulders and accomplishes for the two of us. We have completed our time in New Mexico, we have moved together, sold both of our houses, and are getting ready to move to California.

I have found someone to take over the large number of horses that have been in my care for the last years and I am assured that everyone will be taken care of in the best way possible; they are like my children and I feel responsible for each of them even though they are not mine.

Even publishing this book is in the flow. I had just gotten back the manuscript edited from my dear friend, Dorothy. I had emailed her to thank her for her efforts and time she invested in this and asked her what the next step would be. I was just about to turn away from my computer when I noticed a little square box in the right hand corner of my screen that said: Are you ready to self publish today? Balboa Press Publishing. As I went to research the company I realized that Shambu had told me through someone else a year and a half ago that I would publish a series of books with Hay House Publishing. And literally when I was done with writing and editing it, I was given the next step to take. Publish! And here is the reminder with who you should publish!

Trust always that one step will follow the next and guidance will be given as you move forward in your mission. Sometimes not sooner than needed but just in time! I shall trust this wisdom myself as we are finding just the right place for our Radiant Soul Sanctuary in California and that all will fall into place with finances, moving a rather large amount of animals, household and farm items.

And then again: expect the unexpected! You never know when life might change in a split second, change all your nicely laid out plans and ask for your flexibility, adaptability, surrender and courage to let go. Time is not linear and who can say what happens next?

What a journey this life is! I embrace every part of it and desire for everyone to be able to do the same!

Much love to each of you from the bottom of my heart.

Claudia Mardel

ABOUT THE AUTHOR

Claudia has always loved adventure and travel, not just in her physical form but in a more spiritual sense as well. From a young age she has been looking for the truth—not just her personal truth following her heart wherever it guided her—but for the objective truth that makes the larger picture become whole. Being a very grounded person who loves horses and animals and working with them on a daily basis she has also been gifted with a rare type of sensitivity and intuition that have allowed her to communicate beyond the boundaries of physical existence. When her husband passed away in 2011 she explored this other world and learned to step into her own power and overcome her grief. Her goal is to share her experiences of life, courage, trust and faith with you to help you find your own power and strength within yourself. This has become the work she is doing today.